POET'S CHOICE

EDITED BY

Paul Engle and Joseph Langland

With an Introduction by Paul Engle

TIME Reading Program Special Edition

Time-Life Books Inc., Alexandria, Virginia

Time-Life Books Inc.
is a wholly owned subsidiary of
TIME INCORPORATED

TIME Reading Program: *Editor*, Max Gissen

Library of Congress CIP data following page 291.

For information about any Time-Life book, please write:
Reader Information, Time-Life Books,
541 North Fairbanks Court, Chicago, Illinois 60611

CONTENTS

ACKNOWLEDGMENTS

The authors acknowledge with gratitude the support of the Research Council of the University of Massachusetts in the preparation of the manuscript for this book. The authors also thank Donald Justice for his helpful advice.

FROST, ROBERT: "Choose Something Like A Star" from COMPLETE POEMS OF ROBERT FROST. Copyright 1949 by Holt, Rinehart and Winston, Inc. Reprinted by permission of Holt, Rinehart and Winston, Inc.

WILLIAMS, WILLIAM CARLOS: "The Descent" from DESERT MUSIC AND OTHER POEMS by William Carlos Williams. Copyright 1954 by William Carlos Williams. Reprinted by permission of Random House, Inc.

PRATT, E. J.: "Silences" reprinted from COLLECTED POEMS by E. J. Pratt, by permission of the author and The Macmillan Company of Canada Limited.

WHEELOCK, JOHN HALL: "The Two Societies" (Copyright © 1956 The New Yorker Magazine, Inc.) from POEMS OLD AND NEW by John Hall Wheelock. Reprinted by permission of Charles Scribner's Sons.

JEFFERS, ROBINSON: "To the Stone-Cutters" Copyright 1924 and renewed 1951 by Robinson Jeffers. Reprinted from THE SELECTED POETRY OF ROBINSON JEFFERS, by permission of Random House, Inc. Comment by Robinson Jeffers from "Poetry, Gongorism and A Thousand Years," The New York Times Sunday Magazine, January 18, 1948. Copyright by The New York Times. Reprinted by permission.

MOORE, MARIANNE: "A Face" reprinted with the permission of The Macmillan Company from COLLECTED POEMS by Marianne Moore, Copyright 1951 by Marianne Moore.

RANSOM, JOHN CROWE: "Prelude to an Evening" reprinted from SELECTED POEMS by John Crowe Ransom, by permission of Alfred A. Knopf, Inc. Copyright 1934, 1945 by Alfred A. Knopf, Inc.

AIKEN, CONRAD: "The Walk in the Garden" from A LETTER FROM LI PO by Conrad Aiken. © 1955 by Conrad Aiken and reprinted by permission of Oxford University Press, Inc. Comment by Conrad Aiken from THE CICADO reprinted by permission of Thomas Yoseloff.

MACLEISH, ARCHIBALD: "Words in Time" from COLLECTED POEMS. Reprinted by permission of Houghton Mifflin Company.

CUMMINGS, E. E.: "my father moved through dooms of love" copyright 1940 by E. E. Cummings. Reprinted from POEMS 1923-1954 by E. E. Cummings by permission of Harcourt, Brace & World, Inc.

VAN DOREN, MARK: "Undersong" from MORNING WORSHIP and Other Poems © 1958 by Mark Van Doren. Reprinted by permission of Harcourt, Brace & World, Inc.

GRAVES, ROBERT: "The Troll's Nosegay" from COLLECTED POEMS 1955 Copyright © 1955 by International Authors S. A. Reprinted by permission of Willis Kingsley Wing.

BLUNDEN, EDMUND: "Thoughts of Thomas Hardy" reprinted from SHELLS BY A STREAM by Edmund Blunden by permission of Macmillan & Co. Ltd. and the author.

BOGAN, LOUISE: "Zone" reprinted from COLLECTED POEMS: 1923-53 by Louise Bogan, by permission of Farrar, Straus & Cudahy, Inc. Copyright © 1954 by Louise Bogan.

ADAMS, LEONIE: "Words for the Raker of Leaves" reprinted from POEMS: A SELECTION by permission of Farrar, Straus & Cudahy, Inc. Copyright 1954 by Leonie Adams.

TATE, ALLEN: "The Mediterranean" (Copyright 1933 Yale University Press; renewal copyright © 1961 from POEMS (1960) by Allen Tate. Reprinted by permission of Charles Scribner's Sons.

EDITORS' PREFACE

Few people work harder, or for smaller rewards, than poets, especially American poets. In a country where only half the adults read even one book of any kind a year, the poet is virtually ignored; his books sell badly and usually at a loss to the publisher; his readers sometimes number not many more than the sum total of his fellow poets and their students. There are exceptions, but for every Robert Frost there are dozens of greatly talented and even important poets whose names are virtually unknown to educated people. It may be useless to chide the spirit of the times, but it is worth noting and applauding the fact that poetry refuses to be stilled. What makes *Poet's Choice* a collection of genuine and unusual interest is the diversity of voices that are heard and the variety of reasons given by the poets themselves for their stubborn unwillingness to be quiet.

A good poem is usually an act of discovery, an insight clothed in memorable form and language. Unlike the writer of prose, the poet cannot depend on talent and hard work alone. As John Wain, no great believer in misty "inspiration," puts it so rightly in this book: "I didn't write it — it happened to me. As a professional writer, I can say, 'To-day I will write a story,' or some criticism, or a scene for a play, or whatever it may be: but I cannot say, and no one has ever been able to say, 'To-day I will write poetry.'" It is quite true that a skillful technician, say W. H. Auden, can write about anything under the sun, and on call, in almost any form he chooses. But the chances of its being first-rate poetry would be nearly nil. One of the best critics of poetry (and a fine poet as well), the late Randall Jarrell, stated the odds with rigorous objectivity: "A good poet is someone who manages, in a lifetime of standing out in thunderstorms, to be struck by lightning five or six times; a dozen or two dozen times and he is great."

How many times the lightning strikes in *Poet's Choice* is something that the book makes no attempt to assess. None of the poets either claims greatness or sets it up as a goal. What many of them do attempt is an honest appraisal of the reasons that brought them out into the thunderstorm in the first place, when they might have remained cozy indoors. Honesty, as the distinguished American poet Paul Engle notes in his introduction to this special edition, is one of the hallmarks of the volume; sometimes it is almost painful, as when Theodore Roethke lets the reader share the secret of his marital bliss. Sometimes the poet's prose is inadequate; when John Hollander explains his erudite, elegant and wise "Aristotle to Phyllis," it is possible to wish that the poet had let his verse speak for itself.

There are, however, times when the poems do not manage wholly to explain themselves; at such times the author's comment is invaluable. It would be an uncommon reader, even an uncommon poet, who could guess that Earle Birney's striking poem, "The Bear on the Delhi Road," exposes his Western sense of guilt confronted by the misery he witnessed in India. His poem, and a number of the others, explain two important facts about much of modern poetry. First, a poem can lead a very exciting life of its own in the reader's mind without being literally understood every inch of the way. Second, the lack of clarity, sometimes even the seemingly willful obscurity in much modern poetry is often directly related to poetry's small audience. More than one of the poets here vote for clarity of thought and expression — not prosy simplicity and not "poetic" simple-mindedness and not leading by the hand, but something quite different. David Wagoner makes part of the point: "I dislike poets that swarm around their matter, become too insistent, never seem sure what they have already accomplished but must do it again and again, like a lesser Victorian who has discovered a spring flower and treats it like an all-day sucker. Finally, I most admire poems which have unearthed something of genuine value to the poet himself and, therefore, to anyone willing to go along with him: the symptoms are hard to name but they persuade me."

One thing *Poet's Choice* dispels is precisely the notion that today's poets write only for themselves and for each other. Robert Graves has frequently said that he writes only for other poets, but that can be taken as his way of saying that readers of poetry are so few. Actually there is little or no evidence in this volume of cabals, cliques and closed societies among the poets. There is, to the contrary, so great a range of tone, meaning and sensibility that almost every taste and prejudice in poetry can be touched. Few are the traces of the Imagists of an earlier day who used freedom of form to shroud laziness of mind and absence of discipline. And few are the echoes of the left-wing '30s when a poem without "social significance" had a hard time making its way. There are poems that are prosy, there are poems whose quota of private soul-searching is perhaps excessive. But what is most apparent throughout the book as a whole is a wide streak of intelligence. Not only do the writing skills show that few poets of any age wrote with greater technical virtuosity, but the subject matter and its handling reflect an acuteness of mind that could hardly be found in a similar sampling of today's prose writing. From Conrad Aiken's "The Walk in the Garden," which explores an entire lifetime with extraordinary understanding, to Karl Shapiro's "The Dirty Word" (which should be prescribed reading for some publishers), there is rich evidence of the high intelligence that today's poets seem to value at least as greatly as the poetasters of another day once valued their indifference to it.

Not all the writers have chosen their best poem. Robert Frost for one, Marianne Moore for another, Robert Graves and Robert Lowell, all have failed to do themselves full justice. This in itself, coupled with the reason for the choice, gives a certain insight into the poet's mind and intentions that a critical selection could not achieve. For it soon becomes apparent that there are some things that the poet values beyond the exercise of his skills and, sometimes, even beyond his best grasp as an artist. Thus one values a poem because it celebrates the devotion of his wife, another because he achieved a fitting poem of praise in memory of his father, several because a cherished idea or belief suddenly found itself housed in form and language that seemed totally appropriate. *Poet's Choice* is, in effect, a many-sided view of the poet's vision. Since poetry insists on being written, must be written, it is good to have such a sampler uniting precept and practice.

—THE EDITORS

⟦R⎥P⟧ *INTRODUCTION*

When Joseph Langland and I began to collect the poems in this volume it was with a definite purpose in mind, and with an awareness of certain problems as well. We knew that behind all books of poetry, silent and placid on their shelves, are actual men and women. We knew that their lives are likely to be as intense, if not always as beautiful, as the lines of their poems. We knew something of their attitude toward experience, as the pages of their verse reveal it. But we knew little of their attitude toward their own writing. Would a poet, years after creating a poem, have an affection for it, or would he feel simple indifference? If he did hold a strong feeling about it, would he have the courage to confess that *this* poem, above all others, pleased him?

In an age when the human mind is being examined as never before to see how it really works, would the poets make remarks about their poems which would actually give insights into the creative process? Would they shrug off the writing of a complicated poem as old-fashioned "inspiration," or would they admit honestly that honest work went into it?

We were not, then, simply looking for the poets' personal taste in poetry, interesting as that surely would be. We wanted to learn directly from imaginative men and women how their imaginations took the material of their daily lives and converted it into verse. Finally, we wondered uneasily if poets would be willing to take valuable time away from writing a new poem in order to discuss an older poem which they would never touch again.

The results were more eloquent than we had anticipated. Almost all the poets found the problem a tough one—in John Ciardi's words, "the most demanding and uncomfortable confusion into which I had ever plunged myself." The difficulty was that the poet might have to choose a poem which seemed successful in its form and expression, rather than one which simply had for its origin an experience which he still remembered as deeply moving. Even in the poet's act of choosing, the imagination had to be used.

The poets displayed great personal awareness about their own writing. This is probably the most self-conscious age in history, and it is natural for writers to have a strong sense of self-understanding. Indeed, the very writing of a poem is often a search for realization of the self. In any event, poets, it turned out, *were* willing to speak with candor. It is clear from their responses that the poet finds his own private ordeal merging with the general ordeal of the time; almost every poet included here indicated that he knew full well, often uneasily, what his poem was trying to do. Far more than we had expected, these poets suggested that they were aware of their own feelings and able to shape language to them.

One of the discoveries we made about the creative mind in poetry was this: Writing verse is not the purely intuitive process it was for so long believed to be. Of course the instinctive part of our lives is profoundly at work in all art, but the poet today is convinced that all of his nature, everything that makes him alive, blends into the finished poem. The problem is to keep his feeling and his thinking balanced, so that each strengthens and dramatizes the other.

An astonishing number of poets confessed that they labored over their work in a manner which makes the idea of inspiration seem childish. In his accompanying note, for example, Stephen Spender says "The Generous Years" is the result of "at least 100 attempts"; Kingsley Amis says he rewrote "After Goliath" "so many times I despaired of it."

Despite all the revelations apparent in this volume, the question may yet be asked: Why should anyone, save poets, bother to read a collection of poems and comments on them by the writers? The answer is that life in this part of the 20th Century is sharply reflected in this book. As Alastair Reid notes, the whole purpose of his writing has been "to explore the amazement of finding myself alive." Poem after poem in this volume expresses the amazement of being alive in the middle years of this extreme century. This amazement is not merely wonder that somehow we have avoided that monstrous total destruction whose threat is announced each day when the newspaper lands on our doorstep. It is also the fine and primitive surprise that men feel at the details of their daily living.

Certainly the most moving example of this is found in Philip Levine's poem, "For Fran," and in his comment on it. The poem states in acceptable form, he says, "what no man has a right to say to his wife." For years he wrote poems on the dark disasters of the world; for years his wife coped with children and other domestic affairs. "The price they exacted was enormous, and my wife paid it. She paid it day by day, in her flesh and in her spirit." Finally, he turned and "really looked at her." After that, only this poem could be written. "I had the courage to read her the completed poem. She wept with gratitude. She who never cried in pain wept real tears for these twenty inept lines that celebrate the curse of being a wife."

When we had collected our poems and the poets' explanations, we thus found that we had a double revelation: the poem, telling us what a man or woman felt about a lived-through experience, and the comment, telling us what the poet felt about the experience of writing the poem or the experience of returning to it after some time and deciding that he liked it enough to let it stand for all of his work. And in these accounts of the lives of poets are all our lives.

—PAUL ENGLE

Robert Frost

CHOOSE SOMETHING LIKE A STAR

O Star (the fairest one in sight),
We grant your loftiness the right
To some obscurity of cloud—
It will not do to say of night,
Since dark is what brings out your light.
Some mystery becomes the proud.
But to be wholly taciturn
In your reserve is not allowed.
Say something to us we can learn
By heart and when alone repeat.
Say something! And it says, 'I burn.'
But say with what degree of heat.
Talk Fahrenheit, talk Centigrade.
Use language we can comprehend.
Tell us what elements you blend.
It gives us strangely little aid,
But does tell something in the end.
And steadfast as Keats' Eremite,
Not even stooping from its sphere,
It asks a little of us here.
It asks of us a certain height,
So when at times the mob is swayed
To carry praise or blame too far,
We may choose something like a star
To stay our minds on and be staid.

I am not partial with my poems, any more than a mother with her children. But your choice, "Choose Something Like a Star," is one I like to say.

I seem to fancy it as rather Horatian in its ending. Then I like the two ways of spelling 'staid'; that's playing the words. And I like to mingle science and spirit here—as I do so deliberately in my new book.

But there are things beyond all this which I care more about, and hope we all do.

Robert Frost

William Carlos Williams

THE DESCENT

The descent beckons
        as the ascent beckoned.
                Memory is a kind
of accomplishment,
        a sort of renewal
                even
an initiation, since the spaces it opens are new places
        inhabited by hordes
                heretofore unrealized,
of new kinds—
        since their movements
                are towards new objectives
(even though formerly they were abandoned).

NO DEFEAT is made up entirely of defeat—since
the world it opens is always a place
        formerly
                unsuspected. A
world lost,
        a world unsuspected,
                beckons to new places
and no whiteness (lost) is so white as the memory
of whiteness

WITH EVENING, love wakens
        though its shadows
                which are alive by reason
of the sun shining—
        grow sleepy now and drop away
                from desire....

LOVE WITHOUT shadows stirs now
        beginning to awaken
                as night
advances....

THE DESCENT
        made up of despairs
                and without accomplishment
realizes a new awakening:
                which is a reversal
of despair.
        For what we cannot accomplish, what
is denied to love,
        what we have lost in the anticipation—
                a descent follows,
endless and indestructible....

I write in the American idiom and for many years I have been using what I call the variable foot. "The Descent" is the first poem in that medium that wholly satisfied me.

William Carlos Williams

E. J. Pratt

SILENCES

There is no silence upon the earth or under the earth like
    the silence under the sea;
No cries announcing birth,
No sounds declaring death.
There is silence when the milt is laid on the spawn in the
    weeds and fungus of the rock-clefts;
And silence in the growth and struggle for life.
The bonitoes pounce upon the mackerel,
And are themselves caught by the barracudas,
The sharks kill the barracudas
And the great molluscs rend the sharks,
And all noiselessly—
Though swift be the action and final the conflict,
The drama is silent.

There is no fury upon the earth like the fury under the sea.
For growl and cough and snarl are the tokens of spendthrifts
    who know not the ultimate economy of rage.
Moreover, the pace of the blood is too fast.
But under the waves the blood is sluggard and has the same
    temperature as that of the sea.
There is something pre-reptilian about a silent kill.

Two men may end their hostilities just with their battle-cries.
"The devil take you," says one.
"I'll see you in hell first," says the other.

5

And these introductory salutes followed by a hail of gutturals
and sibilants are often the beginning of friendship, for
who would not prefer to be lustily damned than to
be half-heartedly blessed?
No one need fear oaths that are properly enunciated, for they
belong to the inheritance of just men made perfect, and
for all we know, of such may be the Kingdom of Heaven.
But let silent hate be put away for it feeds upon the heart
of the hater.
Today I watched two pairs of eyes. One pair was black and
the other grey. And while the owners thereof, for the
space of five seconds, walked past each other, the grey
snapped at the black and the black riddled the grey.
One looked to say—"The cat,"
And the other—"The cur."
But no words were spoken;
Not so much as a hiss or a murmur came through the perfect
enamel of the teeth; not so much as a gesture of enmity.
If the right upper lip curled over the canine, it went un-
noticed.
The lashes veiled the eyes not for an instant in the passing.
And as between the two in respect to candour of intention or
eternity of wish, there was no choice, for the stare was
mutual and absolute.
A word would have dulled the exquisite edge of the feeling,
An oath would have flawed the crystallization of the hate.
For only such culture could grow in a climate of silence,—
Away back before the emergence of fur or feather, back to
the unvocal sea and down deep where the darkness spills
its wash on the threshold of light, where the lids never
close upon the eyes, where the inhabitants slay in silence
and are silently slain.

I have chosen "Silences" as representative of ideas and emotions which I have tried to convey throughout my poetry. For almost a generation the sea around the rocky shores of Newfoundland was my daily companion, and its tumultuous beauty, its unpredictable moods, and its devastating cruelty became indelibly impressed upon my mind. Hence the sea has been the central character in most of my lyric and narrative poems.

The drama of life—its conflicts and hostilities, its ironies, and its tragedies—has informed all my poetry: the fierce though wordless struggle between man and beast in the "Cachalot"; between primeval creatures in "The Great Feud"; between man and the sea in "The *Roosevelt* and the *Antinoe*" and "The *Titanic*"; between man and the pristine rocks of earth in my last long poem, "Towards the Last Spike."

"Silences," with its evocation of the mysteries of the fathomless seas, and its enunciation of the epic character of life, no less fierce because constant and casual, is true to the main purposes of my poetry.

E. J. Pratt

John Hall Wheelock

THE TWO SOCIETIES

"Come back at dead of night and speak to me,
You are too much a stranger here—
Come as you used to be,
And have no fear,
My very dear."
"Ah no, that may not be,
To come so near
Is not for you and me."

"O tell me but one thing, for I must know
Or perish of the uncertainty—
Whisper it to me here,
That you are happy so
And we shall meet again." "Ah no,
My very dear.
I may not answer you,
Nor if I answered could you hear."

"The Two Societies" is a dialogue between the living and the dead, and takes its title from Wordsworth's phrase that refers to these as "two great societies." The speakers in the poem could be any two devoted persons, one of whom is no longer living. We may think of them as a husband and wife, separated by the death of the latter.

The man pleads with the woman and she, in some other-worldly existence, is moved, and replies, but more as if speaking to herself, for she knows she cannot reach him, that the dead may not communicate with the living. I have often tried to define what gives this poem so strong a hold upon me. Is it because it seemed almost to write itself and I'm still not sure of its meaning? In any case, I sense that it says a good deal in few words, and its rather complex music, based on four measures of varying length and three recurrent rhymes, has a strangeness I find organic to its mood.

John Hall Wheelock

Robinson Jeffers

TO THE STONE-CUTTERS

Stone-cutters fighting time with marble, you fore-defeated
Challengers of oblivion
Eat cynical earnings, knowing rock splits, records fall down,
The square-limbed Roman letters
Scale in the thaws, wear in the rain. The poet as well
Builds his monument mockingly;
For man will be blotted out, the blithe earth die, the brave
      sun
Die blind and blacken to the heart:
Yet stones have stood for a thousand years, and pained
      thoughts found
The honey of peace in old poems.

Permanent things, or things forever renewed, like the grass and human passions, are the materials for poetry; and whoever speaks across the gap of a thousand years will understand that he has to speak of permanent things, and rather clearly too, or who would hear him?

Robinson Jeffers

Marianne Moore

A FACE

'I am not treacherous, callous, jealous, superstitious,
supercilious, venomous, or absolutely hideous':
    studying and studying its expression,
    exasperated desperation
        though at no real impasse,
        would gladly break the glass;

when love of order, ardour, uncircuitous simplicity,
with an expression of inquiry, are all one needs to be!
    Certain faces, a few, one or two—or one
    face photographed by recollection—
        to my mind, to my sight,
        must remain a delight.

I am very eager while writing—have misgivings, no curiosity after-
wards—no interest in evaluation. Well, one should be obliging. "A
Face" sounds to me like conversation. I do not limit its implication
by saying what face; it is not so long that it overtaxes the attention;
it is positive, an affirmation—not a revenge.

Marianne Moore

John Crowe Ransom

PRELUDE TO AN EVENING

Do not enforce the tired wolf
Dragging his infected wound homeward
To sit tonight with the warm children
Naming the pretty kings of France.

The images of the invaded mind
Being as monsters in the dreams
Of your most brief enchanted headful,
Suppose a miracle of confusion:

That dreamed and undreamt become each other
And mix the night and day of your mind;
And it does not matter your twice crying
From mouth unbeautied against the pillow

To avert the gun of the swarthy soldier,
For cry, cock-crow, or the iron bell
Can crack the sleep-sense of outrage,
Annihilate phantoms who were nothing.

But now, by our perverse supposal,
There is a drift of fog on your mornings;
You in your peignoir, dainty at your orange-cup,
Feel poising round the sunny room

Invisible evil, deprived and bold.
All day the clock will metronome
Your gallant fear; the needles clicking,
The heels detonating the stair's cavern.

Freshening the water in the blue bowls
For the buckberries with not all your love,
You shall be listening for the low wind,
The warning sibilance of pines.

You like a waning moon, and I accusing
Our too banded Eumenides,
You shall make Noes but wanderingly,
Smoothing the heads of the hungry children.

Because it is "pure" as many of this poet's poems are not, in the sense that there is no particular moral or philosophy attaching to it; and because it is open at the end, in the sense that the reader may imagine if he wishes that the speaker by expressing himself has gained some relief, and now is capable of baby-sitting, or whether he has now involved his mate likewise in his own poor spirits. The poem sounds like a "depression" piece of President Hoover's time. The four-beat lines don't count the syllables, nor make rhymes, and that being exceptional pleased the poet. The key to the action is merely the speaker's asking her to "suppose" how it would be for her if her nightmares should suddenly come to haunt her daylight existence. And "Eumenides" are the polite names which the Greeks gave to their Furies.

John Crowe Ransom

Conrad Aiken

THE WALK IN THE GARDEN

I

Noting in slow sequence by waterclock of rain
or dandelion clock of sun
the green hours of trees and white hours of flowers:
annotating again the 'flower-glory of the season,
a book that is never done,' never done:
savoring phrases of green-white, mock-white,
while the ancient lyre-tree, the ancient plum,
adds for another May its solar sum
in silent galaxies of bloom:
it is here, interpreting these, translating these,
stopping in the morning to study these,
touching affectionately the cold bark
of the seven-branched tree, where bees
stir the stars and scatter them down:
it is here, in these whitenesses of thought,
poring over these pages of white thought,
that we ponder anew the lifelong miracle:
the miracle that in these we best remember,
and in wisdom treasure best,
the lost snows of another December,
and the lost heart, and the lost love.
What matter that we are older, that we age?
Blest that we live this morning, blest
that still we read the immortal book
and in time's sunlight turn another page.

II

Shall we call it, then, the walk in the garden?
the morning walk in the simple garden? But only if by this we
mean

everything! The vast daybreak ascends the stairs of pale silver
above a murmur of acacias, the white crowns
shake dark and bright against that swift escalation of light,
and then, in intricate succession, the unfolding minutes and
hours

are marked off by the slow and secret transactions
of ant and grassblade, mole and tree-root,
the shivering cascade of the cicada's downward cry, the
visitation

(when the brazen noon invites) of that lightninged prism
the hummingbird, or the motionless hawkmoth.
Listen! The waterclock of sap in bough and bole,
in bud and twig, even in the dying
branch of the ancient plum-tree, this you hear, and clearly,
at eleven, or three, as the rusted rose-petal
drops softly, being bidden to do so, at the foot of the stem,
past the toad's unwinking eye! Call it
the voyage in the garden, too, for so it is:
the long voyage home, past cape and headland
of the forgotten or remembered: the mystic signal
is barely guessed in the spiderwort's golden eye, recognized
tardily, obscurely, in the quick bronze flash
from the little raindrop left to wither
in the hollow of a dead leaf, or a green fork
of celandine. For in this walk, this voyage,
it is yourself, the profound history of your 'self,'
that now as always you encounter. At eleven or three
it was past these folded capes and headlands, these decisions or
refusals,

these little loves, or great,
that you once came. Did you love? did you hate?
did you murder, or refrain from murder, on an afternoon
of innocent cirrus in April? It is all recorded
(and with it man's history also)
in the garden syllables of dust and dew:
the crucifixions and betrayals,
the lying affirmations and conniving denials,
the cowardly assumptions, when you dared not face yourself,
the little deaths, and the great. Today
among these voluntary resumptions you walk a little way
toward tomorrow. What, then, will you choose to love or hate?
These leaves, these ants, these dews, these steadfast trifles,
                                                    dictate
whether that further walk be little or great.
These waiting histories will have their say.

III
But of those other trifles, the too intrusive,
the factual, the actual, that are too intrusive,
too near, too close, too gross, for deeper meanings:
what of these, what will memory make of these?
Will these too yield in time to the magic of translation?
the bobby-pins, the daily news, the paper-clips, even
the stuffed two-headed calf once seen in a pawnshop window;
as indeed also the crumpled letter, furtively
dropped in the ashcan at the corner,
yes, and the torn half of the movie ticket, bright pink,
found inadvertently in the breast-pocket, to remind you—
but meanly—of other days of afternoon rain:
how will you profitably rehearse these,
how will you (otherwise than here!) rehearse these, and to

                                                    what end

of reconstruction? for what inspired reinterpretation
of the lost image, the lost touch?
Useless, here, the immediate, the factual, the actual:
the telephone remains silent when most you wish to hear it:
the May morning, or is it August or September,
remains empty, infertile, at precisely that instant
when your heart—if that is what you mean by heart—
would invoke a vision.
                              Blessing enough, indeed, it might have been,
but not under peach-tree or lyre-tree,
in the persistence of the radio's tremolo
and the listening silence of an empty room:
blessing enough if in these should quietly have spoken,
in answer to that invocation, that not-voice of voice,
the now almost unknown and unfamiliar voice,
the voice at first not recognized when heard:
blessing enough if in these
indifferent accidents and meaningless impromptus
the angelic not-you should open the door
and angelically enter, to take slow possession
of the room, the chairs, the walls, the windows,
the open piano with its waiting keys,
and the poor bed under the forgotten picture,
but possessing also
the divine touch that in the radiant fingertips
could at once create, with a magician's eloquence,
nothing from something, or something from nothing:
as, out of the untouched piano,
a shabby chord, a threadbare tune, the banal air
squealing from the midnight juke-box, where,
at the corner saloon, over the tepid beer,
you sit and stare,
remembering how the days have become years,

and the minutes hours,
and the false sunlight is distilled to tears
in the sentimental involutions of a shared sound:
yes, and the touch of the fingertip, once, on the back of the
                                                              hand,
or, for a braver instant, tentatively, along the line of the
                                                              cheek:
but no, these are all a broken imagination only,
the one and only heart remains lonely,
the morning remains silent, cannot speak,
muted by the ridiculous trifles, the preposterous trifles,
that stammer between the past and you.
Only, in the thinking hands, for a moment,
the persistent stupid bloodstream vaguely traces—
as if on air, as if on air—
the lost touch, the lost image, the chimerical future:
praying, now, for the illusion of an abstract love.

IV
The illusion of an abstract love? Say, rather,
it was the loves and hates that were illusion,
and all that accompanied them: items of fatigue
or of dubious regret, denials and acceptances,
these it is that are as clouds
gone deathward over the morning, lost, dislimned,
and now recoverable only, if at all,
in the remembered crevice in the remembered garden wall:
abstracted out of space, abstracted out of time,
but now reset, by the morning walk in the garden,
in crystal rhyme.
In these rich leaves, which are not only leaves
of lyre-tree or pomecitron, but also leaves
of a living book that is never done:

from winter to summer, from spring to fall:
in these we keep them all.
Here is that abstract love which we would find
wherein all things become imperishable mind:
the numberless becomes one, the brief becomes everlasting,
the everlasting opens to close
in the perishing of the raindrop on the rose:
violence is understood, and at last still,
evil is fixed and quiet as a tree or hill,
but all alike acceptable and one
and in one pattern made to move, or not to move,
by the illusion, if it is illusion,
of an abstract love.
Touch now again the serpent skin of the lyre-tree:
stoop now again, a hummingbird,
to the magic of the mock-orange:
count again by waterclock of rain
or dandelion clock of sun
the slow days of trees, the quick hours of flowers:
this time, this matin-song, this love, is yours, is ours,
a book that is never done, never done.

What language, this?—The painter's, which is the lover's,
which is the poet's: whose black numbers note
the infinitesimal tick, the monstrous cry.
Grammar and syntax must alike belong
not to the song
but to morphology, the shape that cannot die.

From "The Cicada"

Conrad Aiken

Archibald MacLeish

WORDS IN TIME

Bewildered with the broken tongue
Of wakened angels in our sleep—
Then, lost the music that was sung
And lost the light time cannot keep!

There is a moment when we lie
Bewildered, wakened out of sleep,
When light and sound and all reply:
That moment time must tame and keep.

That moment, like a flight of birds
Flung from the branches where they sleep,
The poet with a beat of words
Flings into time for time to keep.

Some poems know more about their own business than the man who wrote them and go on thinking about it longer than he ever did. This one makes a distinction between time and time which I never intended until I saw it on the page and has gone on ever since making it more and more. I sometimes think the relation between writer and written is reversed here: this poem is writing me.

Archibald MacLeish

E. E. Cummings

my father moved through dooms of love
through sames of am through haves of give,
singing each morning out of each night
my father moved through depths of height

this motionless forgetful where
turned at his glance to shining here;
that if(so timid air is firm)
under his eyes would stir and squirm

newly as from unburied which
floats the first who,his april touch
drove sleeping selves to swarm their fates
woke dreamers to their ghostly roots

and should some why completely weep
my father's fingers brought her sleep:
vainly no smallest voice might cry
for he could feel the mountains grow.

Lifting the valleys of the sea
my father moved through griefs of joy;
praising a forehead called the moon
singing desire into begin

joy was his song and joy so pure
a heart of star by him could steer
and pure so now and now so yes
the wrists of twilight would rejoice

keen as midsummer's keen beyond
conceiving mind of sun will stand,
so strictly (over utmost him
so hugely) stood my father's dream

his flesh was flesh his blood was blood:
no hungry man but wished him food;
no cripple wouldn't creep one mile
uphill to only see him smile.

Scorning the pomp of must and shall
my father moved through dooms of feel;
his anger was as right as rain
his pity was as green as grain

septembering arms of year extend
less humbly wealth to foe and friend
than he to foolish and to wise
offered immeasurable is

proudly and (by octobering flame
beckoned) as earth will downward climb,
so naked for immortal work
his shoulders marched against the dark

his sorrow was as true as bread:
no liar looked him in the head;
if every friend became his foe
he'd laugh and build a world with snow.

My father moved through theys of we,
singing each new leaf out of each tree
(and every child was sure that spring
danced when she heard my father sing)

then let men kill which cannot share,
let blood and flesh be mud and mire,
scheming imagine,passion willed,
freedom a drug that's bought and sold

giving to steal and cruel kind,
a heart to fear,to doubt a mind,
to differ a disease of same,
conform the pinnacle of am

though dull were all we taste as bright,
bitter all utterly things sweet,
maggoty minus and dumb death
all we inherit,all bequeath

and nothing quite so least as truth
—i say though hate were why men breathe—
because my father lived his soul
love is the whole and more than all

follows our nonhero's(prose)"comment"

I choose this poem in the hope that it's not only a portrait of a particular person(one erect generous whole human unique being) but a celebration of the miracle of individuality—by contrast with everything knowable and collective,common and corrupting,cowardly and truthless.

E. E. Cummings

Mark Van Doren

UNDERSONG

1

In wonderment I walk to music pouring
Out of so dark a source it makes no sound:
Not waterfalls, not wind, not eagles soaring
On wings that whistle insult to the ground;
Not insect whine at which the flower rejoices;
Not instruments, not voices;
Not, taciturn, those numbers where they wheel
While the fixed stars, creation's counterpoises,
Sing in deep throats a song of commonweal
More ancient than mankind, than beast or bird
Coeval with the Word:
No, none of these is what I overhear
In wonderment, in walking every day.
A harmony more hidden, as midway
Of the whole world it hums, and yet more near,
More secret in my ear,
Keeps coming to me, coming, and I know
As long as I go forth it shall be so.

2

Each day I walk in is made slyly one
By symmetries whose names I never seek.
For if I did, and found them, and were done
With listening, with looking, and could speak

Love's language with the subtlety they do,
It might no more be true.
For it is music's language, meant to please
No mind except its own, and if I too
Attempted it the melody would cease;
As birds do in the forest if a foot
Too suddenly is put
On pathways saved for silence, or for such
Plumed echoes as are proper to the place.
The music is not mine in any case;
I only let it come, by sight, by touch,
As often as by hearing; though the ghost
Of sound is innermost;
And mightiest, as if the great one there
Had burst his heart and scattered it in air.

3
Down it falls, that wild unfigured tune
Which nevertheless reorders all my earth.
I walk, and every acre is bestrewn
With witnesses of morning in slow birth,
And of the sky's contentment that things be
Just as they are to see.
Different were deadly, something sings
In a low voice as of a leafy tree
Preoccupied with shade, and two sure wings
That aim at it to enter by and by
When the half-day shall die,
And perfect sunlight shall hang due above
Like a dark lantern swinging. Something says,
Barely aloud, in less than sentences:
Just as they are, together in their love,

The whirlwind, the dove,
The contraries. Listen. That rough chord:
It is his breathing, it is our overlord.

4
In times of tempest when disorder seems
Order itself, the very rule of motion,
And moaning as they bend, the trees and streams,
In horror at their own perverse devotion
To chaos come alive, strain not to shatter
Form, and the first matter
Of which all possibility was made;
But then the roar increases, and winds batter
Winds above the world as fields are flayed
And savage grasses, blowing, strip the bones
Even of sunk stones;
In times of tumult when the lines should snap
That lead like silk from note to kissing note,
And the sweet song should strangle in the throat,
There it still is, miles above thunderclap,
As audible as when on halcyon days
It mastered the same ways;
Compounded of all tones, including these
Of stricken ground and hideous green seas.

5
And if there be those who would mock me, saying
"Music? None is here save in your head;
Noises, yes, delectable, dismaying,
But not in measure, as if more were said
Than owls and larks will tell you, or mad crows,
Or the wind-ravished rose,

Or human chatter, changeless year by year;"
Then soberly I say to such as those:
The sound is one, and is not sinister.
It is an honest music through and through.
And so the chatter, too,
And so the silences that wait sometimes
Like a tired giant thinking, so they all
Return and go, then come again and fall,
Evenly, unevenly, as rhymes
Rival the pure chimes
Of never-ending truth, that for so long
Has sung to such as me this undersong.

My favorite as of this moment is "Undersong," partly because
of the formal pleasure I got out of adapting to it the stanza Spenser
used in his "Epithalamion," and partly because of what it says. It
says something quite personal to me, and yet I can think of it as
personal too for anybody else who finds the world, however con-
fusing and terrible it may seem, to be finally intelligible and ac-
ceptable. In my own case I say it is organized as music is. For
others there may be another harmonizing principle. I like to think,
however, that all of those who want to keep on living, as I certainly
do, will understand.

Mark Van Doren

Robert Graves

THE TROLL'S NOSEGAY

A simple nosegay! was that much to ask?
(Winter still nagged, with scarce a bud yet showing.)
He loved her ill, if he resigned the task.
'Somewhere,' she cried, 'there *must* be blossom blowing.'
It seems my lady wept and the troll swore
By Heaven he hated tears: he'd cure her spleen—
Where she had begged one flower he'd shower fourscore,
A bunch fit to amaze a China Queen.

Cold fog-drawn Lily, pale mist-magic Rose
He conjured, and in a glassy cauldron set
With elvish unsubstantial Mignonette
And such vague bloom as wandering dreams enclose.
But she?
      Awed,
           Charmed to tears,
               Distracted,
                    Yet—
Even yet, perhaps, a trifle piqued—who knows?

It is luckiest never to claim a positive value for any poem of your own, but always to say: "Some day, perhaps, if the Muse is kind . . ." Yet an affection often clings to the earliest poem, or the earliest poem printed, or the poem that *She* liked best or . . .

In this sense the one to which I am most attached is "The Troll's Nosegay," written at the close of World War I.

After getting a lung wound—a fragment of shell went right through—I had returned to the trenches too soon and nearly died of bronchitis. Then when, a year later, the Army demobilized me and I rejoined my wife and newly born daughter, I arrived home with so-called "Spanish influenza," alias septic pneumonia, the epidemic that killed twenty million people throughout the world, three times as many as the war itself. My temperature rose to 105, and both lungs were affected. The overworked doctor said I had no chance, the household wept openly, but one thing kept me alive: the obstinate intention of getting my poem right. It had already gone into several drafts, and I wasn't going to be beaten by it. The technical problem was how to make a sonnet read as though it were not a sonnet, while keeping the rules.

By the thirty-fifth draft I had all but solved this, and was tottering about on a stick. "The Troll's Nosegay" saved my life, and I'm grateful. It has since gone into a thirty-sixth, perhaps semifinal, draft. No poem is ever perfected.

Robert Graves

Edmund Blunden

THOUGHTS OF THOMAS HARDY

"Are you looking for someone, you who come pattering
Along this empty corridor, dead leaf, to my door,
And before I had noticed that leaves were now dying?"

"No, nobody; but the way was open.
The wind blew that way.
There was no other way.
And why your question?"

"O, I felt I saw someone with forehead bent downward
At the sound of your coming,
And he in that sound
Looked aware of a vaster threne of decline,
And considering a law of all life.
Yet he lingered, one lovingly regarding
Your particular fate and experience, poor leaf."

O yes, a Favourite Poem. Perhaps "Thoughts of Thomas Hardy," a short one, written while I was busy on a book on him during World War II; written in solitude in the old-fashioned room in Fellows' Quad, Merton College, Oxford, with the corridor outside it, leading to the Garden and Library. All quiet, then a strange dry pattering or footstep-sound from the corridor, out I went. A dead leaf, and it took another step in the autumn gust. It wasn't a ghost! but you remember, Paul, how that region round the Library had some ghostly reputation. So, Thomas Hardy joined me and that brown leaf; and I went back, feeling a little nearer my subject.

Edmund Blunden

Louise Bogan

ZONE

We have struck the regions wherein we are keel or reef.
The wind breaks over us,
And against high sharp angles almost splits into words,
And these are of fear or grief.

Like a ship, we have struck expected latitudes
Of the universe, in March.
Through one short segment's arch
Of the zodiac's round
We pass,
Thinking: Now we hear
What we heard last year,
And bear the wind's rude touch
And its ugly sound
Equally with so much
We have learned how to bear.

"Zone" was written in the later 30's in a transitional period both of my outer circumstances and my central beliefs. It is, therefore, a poem which derives directly from emotional crisis, as, I feel, a lyric must. And I think that the poem's imagery manages to express, in concrete terms (the concrete terms which poetry demands) some reflection of those relentless universal laws, under which we live—which we must not only accept, but in some manner, forgive—as well as the fact of the human courage and faith necessary to that acceptance.

Louise Bogan

Leonie Adams

WORDS FOR THE RAKER OF LEAVES

Birds are of passage now,
Else-wending; where—
Songless, soon gone of late—
They night among us,
No tone now upon grass
Downcast from hedge or grove
With goldener day invites.
Cold, wizening, drear
Lies there the shadowing over.
Yet some, then many from
The blanched net flit and call,
Still a time gambolling,
Into, from the numb skein,
Two, a third with least tune;
And one on the sunned end
Of lawn turns and turns
With rime-dabbled wing.

Air as of two airs
Through day lifts and plays,
In a day that looks away,
Bloom-dappling in the cleft
Of the stone distances
And the dimmed forest weft,
Where, in reddish hues upshed

From about autumnal things,
Shines tenderer, afar seen,
Lastingly after-lit,
Out of all seasons spring;
In a day that looks far
A day that sees plain
Roseate at feet the fresh
Fall of leaf we rake upon
The fallen mouldered brown;
That infiltrate of light
Lace, then, the day pours through,
And the winged seed down-lain.

Clime of two climes
Seems here in time straying,
Its whisperer within sun,
Where, in warm, musing is stood,
And light to the cheek of flesh
All without sifts cool
Upon the sun-warmed one.
Nearer eared than the heard,
Its silences beneath
Of pathos without cry.
In sight fulfilling the eyes,
Vistaed of the beheld
Are its beseechings; wide
Those intimations whence,
Only the offering offering,
Climbs then an eyebeam
To its endless portion;
As it were a vista upon
The suffered and fordone.

I confess to feeling that the more thoroughgoing choice would have been of stanzas, passages, lines; then, that I find it easier to have chosen this lyric than to account for having done so. Turned in at a very late stage in the preparation of my selected poems, it had to displace, as first in the book, another which I well knew would please my readers better. I believe my editor was disconcerted, and I was secretly elated, that she was right, and I was wrong, but not yet that I favor the piece in the sense that one favors a lamed member. In the interim only two or three persons, who had known my work for years, and seemed to me on the whole to have preferred the same titles I did, have ever spoken of it to me. Another of that rare category chose it as one of a group for an anthology, and in the end to my chagrin omitted it. Only one person has ever said he liked it best, and this was an atomic scientist who had been courteous enough to obtain the book, and, he said, read it through, because I was to meet him after a reading.

In its favor I would say that of the later poems yet printed—and let no one expect me to choose one more remote—this is the most songlike and musically structured, and has not jettisoned so much to become so as my earlier attempts in this kind.

But my attachment is more arbitrary, and deeper. I have not outlived, lost, nor seen through the ground of its being. After choosing it, which I did at once, I looked through the selection, as I had not had occasion to do for a long time, and observed something which surprised but did not humiliate me, as it had a lifetime ago, to find out how many times I had used certain words in twenty poems. What I saw was that the earliest pieces not discarded either from my first book or the selection were a twinned first try at working from the same ground and impulse. So with (years later) "The Runner with the Lots," and "Light at Equinox." Once more, the inception of this pair opened for me, after an interval, a long one that time, a period of having some poems to write. So it was with the present piece, again the last of its lot finished, though so easily begun, and even ended. Seven years later, and a little over a year ago, there came to me the initiating movement, an order of images, and a few phrases of another version. Again it was autumn, and though I was in a different and distant landscape, I was in one offering shifts and vistas that seemed as well of time as of space. Again it was for me a time of anxious preoccupation, and what broke in upon habitual burdened thoughts with what seemed a poem out of that very spot in all its strangeness to me, was a very small stir of air about my face. When I have gone back to this, and if I am able to do so (it must be after working at others) have finished it, it will be my favorite among my poems.

Leonie Adam

Allen Tate

THE MEDITERRANEAN

Quem das finem, rex magne, dolorum?

Where we went in the boat was a long bay
A slingshot wide, walled in by towering stone—
Peaked margin of antiquity's delay,
And we went there out of time's monotone:

Where we went in the black hull no light moved
But a gull white-winged along the feckless wave,
The breeze, unseen but fierce as a body loved,
That boat drove onward like a willing slave:

Where we went in the small ship the seaweed
Parted and gave to us the murmuring shore,
And we made feast and in our secret need
Devoured the very plates Aeneas bore:

Where derelict you see through the low twilight
The green coast that you, thunder-tossed, would win,
Drop sail, and hastening to drink all night
Eat dish and bowl to take that sweet land in!

Where we feasted and caroused on the sandless
Pebbles, affecting our day of piracy,
What prophecy of eaten plates could landless
Wanderers fulfil by the ancient sea?

We for that time might taste the famous age
Eternal here yet hidden from our eyes
When lust of power undid its stuffless rage;
They, in a wineskin, bore earth's paradise.

Let us lie down once more by the breathing side
Of Ocean, where our live forefathers sleep
As if the Known Sea still were a month wide—
Atlantis howls but is no longer steep!

What country shall we conquer, what fair land
Unman our conquest and locate our blood?
We've cracked the hemispheres with careless hand!
Now, from the Gates of Hercules we flood

Westward, westward till the barbarous brine
Whelms us to the tired land where tasseling corn,
Fat beans, grapes sweeter than muscadine
Rot on the vine: in that land were we born.

I am not sure that I like this poem better than any other I have
written, but I can return to it occasionally with something that may
faintly resemble pleasure. The imagery is historical and geographical,
and it does not remind me of the difficulties I have had with poems
that seem to have progression "in depth." I wrote the poem very
quickly in 1932 and a few weeks later—at the suggestion of John
Peale Bishop—added a stanza and changed a few phrases. The poem
is obviously in iambic pentameter, but I made a point of not writing
any two lines in the same rhythm. This is a little like the man who
either avoids or steps upon all the cracks in the sidewalk. A great
many of my poems have had to conform to a similar preconceived

technical requirement which does not necessarily have any relation to the subject about to be explored. Even the most serious poems are partly a game, not unlike a child's game, the rules of which are arbitrarily made in advance. I am sorry I misquoted Vergil in the epigraph. I quoted from memory, and unwittingly revised the quotation to make it fit my meaning. The poem ought to be a little longer; and I wish I had made it clear, in the poem, what "eat dish and bowl" means, and not depended upon the reader's knowledge of Vergil.

Allen Tate

Oscar Williams

DWARF OF DISINTEGRATION

I
Who is it runs through the many-storied mansion of myth
With the exaggerated child's-head among pillars and palings,
Holding in his grip the balloons of innumerable windows
And chased by the flowing malevolent army of the ceilings?

It is the dwarf, the yellow dwarf, with the minted cheeks,
With the roots of the fingers, with the wafer-thin cry,
In a maze of walls, lost in the nurseries of definition—
Shadows dance on shins of trumpets in a waning sky.

Voices are wired in the walls, rats are gnawing rumors,
The throat of music is bursting with the leadpipes of lust,
And the giant's face on the dwarf's shoulders is frightened
As the battle sounds strike the panes from the near-by past.

The pillars in the palace are reclining about like pistons:
The horses of parenthesis have run away into the woods:
The king is caught on the vast flypaper of the people:
There are holes as big as hovels in the wall of platitude.

The queen is ill from planting the garden with progeny
And her eyes are crossed off by vicious marks from her face:
She telephones the dwarf who puts his head in the instrument
To find his features come out in glacial coal-bins of space.

The orgasms of distant guns attack at the lustful curtains
And soldiers are standing about in historical knots of lies
Warming frozen tag-ends of lives around the spontaneous
Combustion of bosses who are stoking hollows of hired eyes.

The swine bulge in the snake bellies of the telegraph wires
And bellow under flat clouds of ceilings in the interior;
Communication swallows the quicksilver swords of distance;
Headlines perform, in squadrons of plumes, on the warriors.

But the draughty palace of fable is full of feeble splendor:
The yellow dwarf now in possession of knowing documents
Runs after the newspapers cackling on the edge of freedom—
The golden cupboards tremble for the aging sentiments.

The music of battlefields exhilarates the hidden overhead
And injects into the air a breakdown sense of release,
And the numerals wriggle off the lock boxes of the world
Unloosing a swarm of venomous vultures of the peace.

But the dwarf, the yellow dwarf, with sunspots for eyes
Is hunting in the archives in the moth holes in the palace,
And he tightens the torture boot around the spinal column
The steel twilight gleaming with the sweat of his malice.

II
Now that the battle is on, keep off the palace grounds,
You can hear the dwarf rummaging in the elephant inside:
It's better to draw a curtain of birds around your eyes—
Fall into the picture book under the thumb of a landslide—

Than to come upon spiders eating the iris of the eyeball,
Glimpse the yellow dwarf digesting the members of princes,
Or see famous paintings loll, like tongues, from their frames
Into a roomful of heroes pretending to harass pretenses.

The sagging structure propped between thought and thinker,
The gilded lawns flow on under the smokescreen of the laws:
The allover attack of a decaying body infiltrates to the atom,
Even the beast in the violin hangs out with lopped-off paws.

Run! run into the first thicket of verbs, the nest of deeds!
Place a skyline between yourself and the grandiose emblem!
For the inquisition wears the hypocritical jowls of a palace,
There's nothing here to salvage, and yours is another problem.

It is a weakness of the spirit to rely upon the letter. To ask for
a poet's own favorite poem is a contradiction in terms, calling for
reliance on one "letter to the world" of what should remain a large
and total correspondence. It is tantamount to asking for trouble at
the source. However, since poets, like women, are people and as I
am no exception to this interesting and notoriously soft category,
I shall not resist the temptation, primarily human, of indulging in a
binge of immodesties and arrogances. So here goes: my own favorite
single poem (what poem is ever really single, much less favorite?)
is "Dwarf of Disintegration" for two disparate and desperate reasons.
First, it has a literary history interesting to me personally.

The second reason is that the poem epitomizes, however expan-
sively, the sixteen years I spent in the wilderness of the world try-
ing to make, and alas succeeding in making, a living. (The way to
make a living is by not living!) During that time when I neither read
nor wrote I ransacked the secret and public cellars of society and

discovered they were full of rotted goodies. The shock and revulsion are, I like to believe, thoroughly reflected in the complex imagery of the poem and the simple conclusion it so tortuously reaches. I have no doubt that this poem is a record of some deep trauma. I do not remember the writing of it or of ever having written it. I do not recall thinking of, or *fashioning*, a single one of its numerous aphorisms. It was written through me and in spite of me, without my consent or knowledge or cognizance of college. Hence I am afraid of it and respect it. The Dwarf must be The Yellow Dwarf who terrorized my early years by crawling out of Andrew Lang's *The Yellow Fairy Book* into a painting on the wall of my Unconsciousness. The poem is a door, opening inward, slightly ajar, into that room.

Oscar Williams

Robert Francis

HALLELUJAH: A SESTINA

A wind's word, the Hebrew Hallelujah.
I wonder they never give it to a boy
(Hal for short) boy with wind-wild hair.
It means Praise God, as well it should since praise
Is what God's for. Why didn't they call my father
Hallelujah instead of Ebenezer?

Eben, of course, but christened Ebenezer,
Product of Nova Scotia (hallelujah).
Daniel, a country doctor, was his father
And my father his tenth and final boy.
A baby and last, he had a baby's praise:
Red petticoat, red cheeks, and crow-black hair.

A boy has little say about his hair
And little about a name like Ebenezer
Except that he can shorten either. Praise
God for that, for that shout Hallelujah.
Shout Hallelujah for everything a boy
Can be that is not his father or grandfather.

But then, before you know it, he is a father
Too and passing on his brand of hair
To one more perfectly defenseless boy,

Dubbing him John or James or Ebenezer
But never, so far as I know, Hallelujah,
As if God didn't need quite that much praise.

But what I'm coming to—Could I ever praise
My father half enough for being a father
Who let me be myself? Sing Hallelujah.
Preacher he was with a prophet's head of hair
And what but a prophet's name was Ebenezer,
However little I guessed it as a boy?

Outlandish names of course are never a boy's
Choice. And it takes time to learn to praise.
Stone of Help is the meaning of Ebenezer.
Stone of Help—what fitter name for my father?
Always the Stone of Help however his hair
Might graduate from black to Hallelujah.

Such is the old drama of boy and father.
Praise from a grayhead now with thinning hair.
Sing Ebenezer, Robert, sing Hallelujah!

If you drape thirty-nine iron chains over your arms and shoulders and then do a dance, the whole point of the dance will be to seem light and effortless. Commenting on "Hallelujah: A Sestina," several people said: "We don't know what a sestina is but we enjoy the poem. It made your father vivid." I was both irked and pleased.

It was the first sestina I ever attempted. What made it a little easier was an idea I had before I started. If six words are to be repeated over and over, two things should be true of them: (1) they should be words so "useful" that the ear will keep track of all their recurrences and (2) enjoy the pattern of chiming. Such a word, for instance, as *hallelujah*. That word suggested another Hebrew one, *Ebenezer*. With these two words as a starter, I was on my way. Out of these two words grew everything I found to say.

Yet in starting to write a sestina I was really going against my deepest poetic convictions. For a sestina is an extreme example of a poem written from the outside in, and my way is to write from the inside out. To encourage a poem, as it grows, to grow its own skeleton and skin. Like a living cat. And not to start with the skin, as the taxidermist does, and stuff it out. I am strong for form, but not for forms. Perhaps I should now admit that a poem written the wrong way may sometimes be more successful than a poem written the right way.

I have no favorite poem or poems. Enough to say that this poem is one of peculiar interest to me.

Robert Francis

Langston Hughes

BORDER LINE

I used to wonder
About living and dying—
I think the difference lies
Between tears and crying.

I used to wonder
About here and there—
I think the distance
Is nowhere.

"Border Line" is one of my favorite poems because it seems to carry within itself a melody which I can hear although I cannot sing a note. Since this poem is like a song, its sound conditioned its saying. *What* it says is therefore so much of a piece with the way it is said that form and content are one, like a circle whose shape is itself and whose self is its shape, and which could be no other way to be what it is. I did not consciously compose this poem. It came to me, and I simply wrote it down, and wondered where it came from, and liked it. Possibly I like it because it was not contrived, inception having been outside myself.

Langston Hughes

Brewster Ghiselin

ANSWERING A LETTER FROM A YOUNGER POET

I
What shall I say but, having written for use,
I am glad, hearing that others shape, with words
Made for my ear and stride, a life like mine.
To await the recommendation of death
Is to tell oneself secrets, like the mad.

Gregarious man, the loneliest animal,
Varying even from himself always,
Many envy the conclusion of the dove
The brutal seasons charm, daylong aloft
In his high cool defined and redefined:
The invariable being of a bird.

I think of the young, who must think much of war,
Little of being. But will find in wars
A unison (their anguish) nearly love's.

II
Lawrence and Bishop were the men I chose,
Because they made of momentary ways
Their being. All their light walked over water

And sought a man commensurate with light
And found him multiple as the glassy ghost
Of Proteus we wrestle in the sea.

How shall we endure change? Swimmers who deal
With shadows subtler than the octopus,
Who brave what nicors died in Beowulf's boast
And dare the shoaling combers' cold turbines
Yet tire of the open, ride inshorings, wade,
Look to the land where happier beings close
Hand upon hand or blade to know themselves,
Far from the garden of the waves' whitening rose.

Meditating changes in a stone
I think of dust, that scared stone-worshipers
Of water, where even dust is dimmed or lost;
Of dark, gathering that turbulence.
And know why Bishop painted a green dawn
And praised its wind, how in the salt of touch
Those men divined a measure, then a thought.

III
Twenty-five years ago alone in foam
Between the brown and blue of noon I climbed
The hill of change in instantaneous flame
Up the thrown slope of an enormous wave
To a height toppling like a bathing swan.

A wave like Paradise. On the small sand
Love in a stillness watched the wide ocean.
Poised between love and death, I seemed to choose
The shore. But I chose both: fury of change,
Earth and ocean, furies of a man.

49

I have found no definition of a man
But in that change, where now you hear and move.
Even in that loneliest wave we are not alone.

In poetry, as in all experience, I desire neither rigidity nor muddle, but rather a perfect definiteness, of shape and movement, that never falls into finality. Therefore, I prefer a poetry more concrete than abstract, in which all the parts are at play with one another—a design as restless as waves, a design that never freezes. Fear and inertia make us want to repose in conclusions, to come to rest finally in certain insights, modes of being, and ways of behaving. Settling down in the safety and comfort thus provided, we find ourselves among structures that we cannot live by. And our faith in them decays. We change despite ourselves, helplessly, passively, and in terror. Life is wholly maintainable only through shifting our positions and perspectives, by fostering the variations of subjective being, the transformations of spirit, and the transactions of insight through which we envisage reality and deal with occasions. Yet it is hard to embrace this necessity, even part of the time. My poem "Answering a Letter from a Younger Poet" interests me because in examining this necessity, its nature, the difficulty of facing it, and the pains and delights involved in submitting to it, I am learning to understand and accept the best of my own experience.

Brewster Ghiselin

Ogden Nash

THE PRIVATE DINING ROOM

Miss Rafferty wore taffeta,
Miss Cavendish wore lavender.
We ate pickerel and mackerel
And other lavish provender,
Miss Cavendish was Lalage,
Miss Rafferty was Barbara.
We gobbled pickled mackerel
And broke the candelabara,
Miss Cavendish in lavender,
In taffeta, Miss Rafferty,
The girls in taffeta lavender,
And we, of course, in mufti.

Miss Rafferty wore taffeta,
The taffeta was lavender,
Was lavend, lavender, lavenderest,
As the wine improved the provender.
Miss Cavendish wore lavender,
The lavender was taffeta.
We boggled mackled pickerel,
And bumpers did we quaffeta.
And Lalage wore lavender,
And lavender wore Barbara,
Rafferta taffeta Cavender lavender
Barbara abracadabra.

Miss Rafferty in taffeta
Grew definitely raffisher.
Miss Cavendish in lavender
Grew less and less stand-offisher.
With Lalage and Barbara
We grew a little pickereled,
We ordered Mumm and Roederer
Because the bubbles tickereled.
But lavender and taffeta
Were gone when we were soberer.
I haven't thought for thirty years
Of Lalage and Barbara.

From a thirty-three year high mountain of trivia I offer this mouse.
    I have chosen "The Private Dining Room" because I took partic-
ular pleasure in putting it together, and because it has evoked kind
words from several poets whom I admire.

Ogden Nash

Earle Birney

THE BEAR ON THE DELHI ROAD

Unreal, tall as a myth
by the road the Himalayan bear
is beating the brilliant air
with his crooked arms.
About him two men, bare,
spindly as locusts, leap.
One pulls on a ring
in the great soft nose; his mate
flicks, flicks with a stick
up at the rolling eyes.

They have not led him here,
down from the fabulous hills
to this bald, alien plain
and the clamorous world, to kill
but simply to teach him to dance.

They are peaceful both, these spare
men of Kashmir, and the bear
alive is their living, too.
If far on the Delhi way
around him galvanic they dance
it is merely to wear, wear
from his shaggy body the tranced

wish forever to stay
only an ambling bear
four-footed in berries.

It is no more joyous for them
in this hot dust to prance
out of reach of the praying claws
sharpened to paw for ants
in the shadows of deodars.
It is not easy to free
myth from reality
or rear this fellow up
to lurch, lurch with them
in the tranced dancing of men.

The only poems of mine I wholeheartedly like are the ones I'm still hoping to write. However, this piece doesn't bore me yet, and disappoints me a little less than the others I've written and done with. Why? Do I know? I think it escapes some faults I'm prone to: rhetoric, lumpiness, diffusion; but that's only a negative reason. It's partly that it laid a particularly nagging ghost, one that followed me from the Cangetic plain (where it started up, in a flash) until I exorcised it on a Mediterranean island more than a year later. But the scene of the exorcism is important too—for me only. I remember the way the rhythm came of itself and possessed me all that shining day, and the girl who waited under the dappled fig arbor while I got the first draft penciled, and then raced me in for a long swim in the August sea, and my huge hunger after, and langoustines, and talk of Erich Fromm, and other things highly important for the writing of the poem, and totally irrelevant for the reading of it.

Most of all I think I am grateful to this poem for lessening a feeling of guilt within me. The summer before, I had spent five weeks in India. I'd never been in Asia before, then, suddenly—five weeks in the heart of it. I'm still only a grown-up Alberta ranch boy, and I was drowned in strangeness, objects unthought of, people unimagined: the hollow tombs and the seething streets, the empty peace of a houseboat in the Vale of Kashmir, a child left to die of cholera on the banks of the Jumna, cocktails at an embassy, the sun battering on Gandhi's tomb. And always the presence of the poor, the millions upon millions of incredibly poor, sick or half well, infants or old-men-of-thirty. And the need to say something to encompass them, and the sense of shame in not finding a way to say anything.

Of course I've not shaken off my guilt here, for that is lodged in something deeper even than my conscience as a writer, in that uneasy *imago* of myself as an over-privileged Western man. But I have, in this poem, worked from a sudden vision of a reality otherwise inexpressible for me into an expression of some small part of that compassion and fear and love and despair that overwhelmed me when I was in India. Perhaps I managed also to evoke something about the oddness of Myth, but if so it was accidental. I'm grateful enough to have appeased one of my thronging ghosts.

C. Day Lewis

THE ROOM

For George Seferis

To this room—it was somewhere at the palace's
Heart, but no one, not even visiting royalty
Or reigning mistress, ever had been inside it—
To this room he'd retire.
Graciously giving himself to, guarding himself from
Courtier, suppliant, stiff ambassador,
Supple assassin, into this unviewed room
He, with the air of one urgently called from
High affairs to some yet loftier duty,
Dismissing them all, withdrew.

And we imagined it suitably fitted out
For communing with a God, for meditation
On the Just City; or, at the least, a bower of
Superior orgies . . . He
Alone could know the room as windowless
Though airy, bare yet filled with the junk you find
In any child-loved attic; and how he went there
Simply to taste himself, to be reassured
That under the royal action and abstraction
He lived in, he was real.

I have chosen this poem partly because it is the last one I have written, and I always want the last one I have written to be my best, and generally it seems my best—for a few hours, or even days, after I have written it.

I also like it because it is a profoundly personal poem which reads (I hope) like an impersonal one. It began with the phrase "to taste himself"; what it is saying, from the personal point of view, is that I, like almost every elderly poet in England, have become involved willy-nilly in activities—committees, lectures, public stances—which have little to do with making poems, and which tend to diminish my reality, or at least my feeling of being real. The room the King goes into is his solitude, his sanctum—the part of him inviolate from public preoccupations, uncorrupted by public business.

But of course the poem should have a similar meaning—about solitude and integrity—for any man or woman. If it has not, but is interpreted simply as yet another poem about "the poet's predicament in the modern world," or some such boring specialised subject —then it is worthless.

Perhaps a better reason for choosing it is that Seferis, whom I believe to be the greatest living European poet, let me dedicate it to him.

C Day Lewis

Richard Eberhart

ON A SQUIRREL CROSSING THE ROAD IN AUTUMN, IN NEW ENGLAND

It is what he does not know,
Crossing the road under the elm trees,
About the mechanism of my car,
About the Commonwealth of Massachusetts,
About Mozart, India, Arcturus,

That wins my praise. I engage
At once in whirling squirrel-praise.

He obeys the orders of nature
Without knowing them.
It is what he does not know
That makes him beautiful.
Such a knot of little purposeful nature!

I who can see him as he cannot see himself
Repose in the ignorance that is his blessing.

It is what man does not know of God
Composes the visible poem of the world.
                              . . . Just missed him!

I like the Squirrel poem because it is one of two, the other being "The Cancer Cells," which I have written directly after the experience which caused the poem. There is something deeper than immediacy of perception and this poem, then, is not typical of the origins of most of my poems. However, it has met with warm response from audiences, is short, and has also an untypical half-line at the end.

When I almost hit the squirrel I pulled over to the right, stopped in a ditch, and experienced a period of nervosity or illumination during which I felt clairvoyant. This lasted probably several minutes. I felt I knew and possessed, that is, experienced all possible relationships between the small squirrel, myself as a slightly larger animal, and the immense idea of God. I was conscious of fate and time. I happened to have an envelope in my pocket and a pencil. If I had not had these immediately to hand I would have lost the poem. I wrote it down at once.

I have a special affection for it, then, because an event in nature immediately produced a poem and because this method of composition is unusual with me, alien to my usual modes of being, thought, and feeling, an upwelling into consciousness of relationships having nothing to do directly with experience, but coming out of reservoirs of memory from mysterious promptings, promptings of delicate and strong balances fashioning the created harmonies of poems.

Richard Eberhart

John Holmes

A WILLING SUSPENSION

John Milton said the world in a starry rain
Was hung from heaven's floor by a golden chain,
And would not be displaced and could not fall.
We think the world is held by its own spin
Where it is, and will be, and has always been,
Though we make burns and gouges in the ball.

Milton by Galileo could have been told
World depends from no stranded loops of gold,
But had his poem to make, and would not hear.
I hang, and I have always known I hung
From the floor of heaven, and when I was young
Rattled my golden chain and golden sphere.

Hang is the word for it still, hard to the floor's
Underside, though cratered by meteors.
What was cable I see is old-fashioned rope,
Or cord. It could be called cord, but it's thread
I'll be hanged with by the neck now till I'm dead.
From the bump of wars and nicks of time I look up

At that thin thread. Is that all it is?
The man next door at eighty dangles on his,
Less than twice my age, and holds up well,
Classicist and grandfather. Where do they get stuff
Like that, stone-thread, sun-wire, thong so tough
I feel safe from my own or even Milton's hell?

Someone told my wife, who told me, of a doctor who remarked
to a patient that the thread life seems to hang by is a very tough
thread. Without wholly understanding it, or being quite sure a poem
should come this way, accidental and unexpected reminders of deep
feelings I have long had, give me the poems I like best to have writ-
ten. I do not conspire or prearrange, and I enjoy the surprises of
memory and excited composition. So I remembered a Milton course
in college, and thinned the golden chain down through the years of
my life to the tough thread we say we hang by.

I want my poems to come as close to the brooding, pervasive,
local but universalized forces of life as I can make them come. I see
that I most often do it subjectively, in a half-narrative. I want ob-
jects in my poems, a main image to be remembered, the poem about
my brother, the poem about the back yard, about the country fire-
truck, or about how to listen well. Once a student said my poems
are filled with the sad love of humanity, and sadly and lovingly I
accept this, but with exultation, too.

I liked the way "A Willing Suspension" came out, in form and
rhyme. However much I vary tone, line length, and shape of a poem,
I want to get one I can read aloud in my own most natural speaking
voice, but emotionally heightened. This one works this way for me.
Now nothing less than the bite, salt, compassion, and love I mean
in this poem satisfies me any more, and I know that since I wrote it, I
have had a breakthrough that is still more deeply satisfying. As an
intuitive and outwardly reticent person, I can say more raging, more

loving, more cherishing things in poems than ever face to face. I think the poet wants to be understood for himself, in a guileless and selfishly unselfish dream of furthering all understanding, each of himself and all of all others.

John Holmes

Patrick Kavanagh

IMPORTANT STATEMENT

In Islington for the moment I reside,
A hen's race from Cheapside
Where Tom the peeping sun first eyed—

Where Gilpin's horse had bolted
And all the traffic halted,
The man aboard was malted.

And in these romantic spots
I run into Paul Potts
Feeling the pull of roots.

I have taken roots of love
And will find it pain to move . . .
Betjeman, you've missed much of

The secrets of London while
Old churches you beguile,
I'll show you a holier aisle

The length of Gibson Square
Caught in November's stare,
That would set you to prayer.

Dickens—all the old clichés
Revert to their natural species,
Ideas with the impact of Nietzsche's.

I walk in Islington Green,
Finer landscape you never seen,
I'm as happy as I've ever been.

I enjoyed writing "Important Statement," and I enjoy it still for
reasons that have not much to do with poetics—or at least are not
supposed to have. First, its inconsequence. It is an Important State-
ment because it is of no importance. Most attempts at autobiography
are choked by their importance, the disastrous "I am." To be suc-
cessful we must be gay and indifferent and forget who we are. To a
certain extent it is the lack of the right sympathy in an audience
which causes this lockjaw.

The second reason for my pleasure is similar to the first. Over the
past few years—since about 1956—I have learned the magical, imag-
ination-stimulating quality of outrageous rhyming: clichés, species,
Nietzsche's.

My third pleasure comes from this: I wrote the poem on a Tuesday.
I took the bus the short ride into the offices of the *Observer* in Lon-
don. Next day, at noon, I went back to the *Observer*, where I got my
fee, which was something around fifty dollars. The poem was pub-
lished the next Sunday. There is something highly pleasing about
getting oneself out of a financial hole by a poem. I mean for a poet.

Finally, Islington, in North London, is an old part of the city, filled
with echoes of the eighteenth and nineteenth centuries. Lovely little
coloured houses and small narrow squares. But I'm getting in danger
of getting important, guidebook seriousness. That would be awful.

Patrick Kavanagh

Stanley Kunitz

THE DARK AND THE FAIR

A roaring company that festive night;
The beast of dialectic dragged his chains,
Prowling from chair to chair in the smoking light,
While the snow hissed against the windowpanes.

Our politics, our science, and our faith
Were whiskey on the tongue; I, being rent
By the fierce divisions of our time, cried death
And death again, and my own dying meant.

Out of her secret life, that griffin-land
Where ivory empires build their stage, she came,
Putting in mine her small impulsive hand,
Five-fingered gift, and the palm not tame.

The moment clanged; beauty and terror danced
To the wild vibration of a sister-bell,
Whose unremitting stroke discountenanced
The marvel that the mirrors blazed to tell.

A darker image took this fairer form
Who once, in the purgatory of my pride,
When innocence betrayed me in a room
Of mocking elders, swept handsome to my side,

Until we rose together, arm in arm,
And fled together back into the world.
What brought her now, in the semblance of the warm,
Out of cold spaces, damned by colder blood?

That furied woman did me grievous wrong,
But does it matter much, given our years?
We learn, as the thread plays out, that we belong
Less to what flatters us than to what scars;

So, freshly turning, as the turn condones,
For her I killed the propitiatory bird,
Kissing her down. Peace to her bitter bones,
Who taught me the serpent's word, but yet the word.

Among my reasons for choosing "The Dark and the Fair": (1) I like a poem that rides the beast of an action, (2) I can still read it without flinching, (3) I doubt that I could make it any better by tinkering with it, (4) perhaps there is some wisdom in it along with all that folly.

When I am asked to comment on what happens in this poem, I can think of nothing to say except that of the two women who are being celebrated here, it is the "dark" one, risen from the past, who eventually usurps the scene. As a dramatic lyric, the poem is meant to be read aloud—indeed this could be said of most of my work.

After I first published the poem, in the late fifties, a stranger wrote to me that there were lines in it that "beat the hell" out of him . . . the best praise I ever heard. I have his generous letter, dated October 1, 1958, before me as I write, and I am disarmed again by the fresh candor of my correspondent's voice, as in his offer of an interpretation: " 'The Dark and the Fair,' it seems to me, is the story of a love affair and also, how Art came to you." In a passage that follows he incorporates his stage directions: ". . . after the first two stanzas, which I read with an obvious energy, I pause for about three seconds; then I begin pianissimo with 'Out of her secret life' and build to a quiet sustained, intense thing ending on 'colder blood.' I pause for about four seconds and resign (*sic*) proudly for the rest of the way."

And now it seems clear to me that my final reason for choosing this poem is that it was favored by Anthony Bove of Pittsburgh, Pennsylvania, stone mason and poet, who died untimely in Madrid at the age of twenty-eight.

Stanley Kunitz

E. L. Mayo

VARIATIONS ON A LINE FROM SHAKESPEARE'S FIFTY-SIXTH SONNET

Watched and well-known to the police, he walks
The Garden of the Oil Press. The great trees
Sweat in the mist, their moisture-swollen trunks
Fleshlike to touch. The cup
Of nausea for man being filled up
And emptied now, he goes
To wake eleven sleepers
Lest they lack sight to see Iscariot close
As lithely as a springe for garroting sparrows.

This is the man.   This is the arch-traitor
To land   bread   progress   family
Israel   Rome   and every other power

Whose action is stronger than a flower,

In time and just in time turning the minor
World we live on like some lost airliner
Back to the course direct, till every eye
Center by two crossed sticks stuck in a skull
Between a criminal and a criminal
The power

Whose action is no stronger than a flower.

I remember the writing of this poem because it proved particularly difficult to do. I knew what I wanted, but revision followed revision without any prospect of finality—and then suddenly everything snapped into shape. Most poems with an overtly religious orientation come hard these days, at least they do for me. Why? Chiefly, I suspect, because most poems are the outcome, at one level or another, of a sort of rapport between the personal feelings of the poet and the spirit of the age in which he lives. And in our age the religious poem must be written as it were against the grain of the *Zeitgeist*.

Reading it over today, I was struck by the miscellaneity of the elements of the poem. In the final section, for example, I recognize a reflection of my long fealty to Science Fiction (or should one call it *anti*-science fiction?). More important is my deep-seated antipathy to compulsion of every kind in a world where political, social, economic, and "religious" pressures clamp ever more insistently on the individual. There was the realization too that for his compatriots not Jesus but Judas was the exemplary citizen, the man who in spite of powerful temptations ultimately did the Right Thing by Church and State.

Of course I realize that the magnificent line from Shakespeare outshines all the rest; yet I hope and believe that by putting it in this context I have given it a new dimension and so justified my use of it.

E. L. Mayo

Phyllis McGinley

BALLADE OF LOST OBJECTS

Where are the ribbons I tie my hair with?
   Where is my lipstick? Where are my hose—
The sheer ones hoarded these weeks to wear with
   Frocks the closets do not disclose?
Perfumes, petticoats, sports chapeaux,
   The blouse Parisian, the earring Spanish—
Everything suddenly ups and goes.
   And where in the world did the children vanish?

This is the house I used to share with
   Girls in pinafores, shier than does.
I can recall how they climbed my stair with
   Gales of giggles, on their toptoes.
Last seen wearing both braids and bows
   (But looking rather Raggedy-Annish),
When they departed nobody knows—
   Where in the world did the children vanish?

Two tall strangers, now I must bear with,
   Decked in my personal furbelows,
Raiding the larder, rending the air with
   Gossip and terrible radios.

Neither my friends nor quite my foes,
    Alien, beautiful, stern, and clannish,
Here they dwell, while the wonder grows:
    Where in the world did the children vanish?

Prince, I warn you, under the rose,
    Time is the thief you cannot banish.
These are my daughters, I suppose.
    But where in the world did the children vanish?

I choose "Ballade of Lost Objects." I value it for two reasons:
    First, it is a skillful ballade, that rather stereotyped French form which is so often merely a catalogue. This poem, I like to think, *progresses*—it utilizes the rather stiff metrical design to achieve a mood and an emotion. I love verse-skills and feel I have demonstrated here that ornamental forms can carry a certain weight of thought and poignancy.
    Second, it is a woman's piece of verse. And as there are masculine virtues, there are female ones also. The human pathos of having one's children grown up and past their homes is as full of truth as, say, a tragic love affair—and much more frequent.

Phyllis McGinley

Robert Penn Warren

MORTMAIN

1. After Night Flight Son Reaches Bedside of Already
Unconscious Father, Whose Right Hand Lifts
In A Spasmodic Gesture, As Though Trying
To Make Contact: 1955

*

In Time's concatenation and
Carnal conventicle, I,
Arriving, being flung through dark and
The abstract flight-grid of sky,
Saw rising from the sweated sheet and
Ruck of bedclothes ritualistically
Reordered by the paid hand
Of mercy—saw rising the hand—

*

Christ, start again! What was it I,
Standing there, travel-shaken, saw
Rising? What could it be that I,
Caught sudden in gut- or conscience-gnaw,
Saw rising out of the past, which I
Saw now as twisted bedclothes? Like law,
The hand rose cold from History
To claw at a star in the black sky,

But could not reach that far—oh, cannot!
And the star horribly burned, burns,
For in darkness the wax-white clutch could not
Reach it, and white hand on wrist-stem turns,
Lifts in last tension of tendon, but cannot
Make contact—oh, *oop-si-daisy*, churns
The sad heart, *oh, atta-boy, daddio's got*
One more shot in the locker, peas-porridge hot—

*

But no. Like an eyelid the hand sank, strove
Downward, and in that darkening roar,
All things—all joy and the hope that strove,
The failed exam, the admired endeavor,
Prizes and prinkings, and the truth that strove,
And back of the Capitol, boyhood's first whore—
Were snatched from me, and I could not move,
Naked in that black blast of his love.

2. A Dead Language: Circa 1885
Father dead, land lost, stepmother haggard with kids,
Big Brother skedaddling off to Mexico
To make his fortune, gold or cattle or cards,
What could he do but what we see him doing?
Cutting crossties for the first railroad in the region,
Sixteen and strong as a man—was a man, by God!—
And the double-bit bit into red oak, and in that rhythm,
In his head, all day, marched the Greek paradigm:
That was all that was his, and all he could carry all day with
    him.

                              :   and the axe swung.
That was that year, and the next year we see him
Revolve in his dream between the piece goods and cheese,
In a crossroads store, between peppermint candy and
    plow-points,
While the eaves drip, and beyond the black trees of winter
Last light grays out, and in the ruts of the lane
Water gleams, sober as steel. That was that land,
And that was the life, and he reached out and
Took the dime from the gray-scaled palm of the Negro
    plowhand's hand.

*

                              :   in the beginning
Was the word, but in the end was
What?   At the mirror, lather on chin, with a razor
Big as a corn-knife, or so to the boy it seemed,
He stood, and said:
And laughed. And said: "That's Greek, now you know how
    it sounds!"
And laughed, and waved the bright blade like a toy.
And laughing from the deep of a dark conquest and joy,
Said: "Greek—but it wasn't for me. Let's get to breakfast,
    boy."

3. Fox-Fire: 1956

Years later, I find the old grammar, yellowed.   Night
Is falling.   Ash flakes from the log.   The log
Glows, winks, wanes.   Westward, the sky
In one small area redeemed from gray, bleeds dully.
Beyond my window, athwart that red west,

The spruce bough, though snow-burdened, looks black,
Not white.   The world lives by the trick of the eye, the trick
Of the heart.   I hold the book in my hand, but God
—In what mercy, if mercy?—will not let me weep. But I
Do not want to weep.   I want to understand.

*

Oh, let me understand what is that sound,
Like wind, that fills the enormous dark of my head.
Beyond my head there is no wind, the room
Darkening, the world beyond the room darkening,
And no wind beyond to cleave, unclot, the thickening
Darkness.   There must be a way to state the problem.
The statement of a problem, no doubt, determines solution.
If once, clear and distinct, I could state it, then God
Could no longer fall back on His old alibi of ignorance.
I hear now my small son laugh from a farther room.

*

I know he sits there and laughs among his toys,
Teddy bear, letter blocks, yellow dump truck, derrick,
    choo-choo—
Bright images, all, of Life's significance.
So I put the book on the shelf, beside my own grammar,
Unopened these thirty years, and leave the dark room,
And know that all night, while the constellations grind,
Beings with folded wings brood above that shelf,
Awe-struck and imbecile, and in the dark,
Amid History's vice and velleity, that poor book burns
Like fox-fire in the black swamp of the world's error.

4. In the Turpitude of Time: N.D.

In the turpitude of Time,
Hope dances on the razor edge.
I see those ever-healing feet
Tread the honed edge above despair.
I see the song-wet lip and tossing hair.

*

The leaf unfolds the April weather.
The heart spills the horizon's light.
In the woods, the hunter, weeping, kneels,
And the dappled fawn weeps in contrition
For its own beauty.   I hear the toad's intercession

*

For us, and all, who do not know
How cause flows backward from effect
To bless the past occasion, and
How Time's tongue lifts only to tell,
Minute by minute, what truth the brave heart will fulfill.

*

Can we—oh, could we only—believe
What annelid and osprey know,
And the stone, nightlong, groans to divulge?
If we could only, then that star
That dawnward slants might sing to our human ear,

*

And joy, in daylight, run like feet,
And strength, in darkness, wait like hands,

76

And between the stone and the wind's voice
A silence wait to become our own song:
In the heart's last kingdom only the old are young.

5. A Vision: Circa 1880
Out of the woods where pollen is a powder of gold
Shaken from pistil of oak minutely, and of maple,
And is falling, and the tulip tree lifts, not yet tarnished,
The last calyx, in which chartreuse coolness recessed, dew,
Only this morning, lingered till noon—look,
Out of the woods, barefoot, the boy comes. He stands,
Hieratic, complete, in patched britches and that idleness of
    boyhood
Which asks nothing and is its own fulfilment:
In his hand a wand of peeled willow, boy-idle and aimless.

*

Poised between woods and the pasture, sun-green and green
    shadow,
Hair sweat-dark, brow bearing a smudge of gold pollen, lips
Parted in some near-smile of boyish bemusement,
Dangling the willow, he stands, and I—I stare
Down the tube and darkening corridor of Time
That breaks, like tears, upon that sunlit space,
And staring, I know who he is, and would cry out.
Out of my knowledge, I would cry out and say:
Listen! Say: *Listen! I know—oh, I know—let me tell you!*

*

That scene is in Trigg County, and I see it.
Trigg County is in Kentucky, and I have been there,
But never remember the spring there. I remember

A land of cedar-shade, blue, and the purl of lime-water,
But the pasture parched, and the voice of the lost joree
Unrelenting as conscience, and sick, and the afternoon throbs,
And the sun's hot eye on the dry leaf shrivels the aphid,
And the sun's heel does violence in the corn-balk.
That is what I remember, and so the scene

*

I had seen just now in the mind's eye, vernal,
Is altered, and I strive to cry across the dry pasture,
But cannot, nor move, for my feet, like dry corn-roots, cleave
Into the hard earth, and my tongue makes only the dry,
Slight sound of wind on autumn corn-blades. The boy,
With imperial calm, crosses a space, rejoins
The shadow of woods, but pauses, turns, grins once,
And is gone. And one high oak leaf stirs gray, and the air,
Stirring, freshens to the far favor of rain.

We all know that the poet's personal feelings and convictions enter somehow into his poem. But we know, too, that the strictly personal adequacy of the expression—the cathartic value for the poet, we might say—has nothing to do with the value of a poem. For the poem is a thing made, made according to the laws of the art which it professes to represent; and once made, it stands apart from, though yet absorbing, even dramatizing, whatever human urgencies were involved in the making. The human urgencies, of which in varying degrees we remain conscious in any poem, are absorbed into the depersonalizing form—with its paradox of continually recapitulated urgency and fulfilment.

The poem I have chosen here is, clearly, personal. Further, the personal urgencies are dramatized, are overtly presented, not merely absorbed. In such a poem the writer runs his greatest risks—among those risks, the most risky risk of self-deception, self-deception about the feelings themselves and self-deception about the transmutation of those feelings.

I have chosen this poem because it involves those risks, because, particularly in "After Night Flight," I felt somehow impelled to compound the risks. This is the kind of poem I have felt impelled, more and more in late years, though for reasons that are not clear to me, to try. If this poem succeeds in being a poem, it is the kind of poem I now should most like to write. If it fails, it remains, at least, representative.

John Betjeman

POT-POURRI FROM A SURREY GARDEN

Miles of pram in the wind and Pam in the gorse track.
　　Coco-nut smell of the broom, and a packet of Weights
Press'd in the sand. The thud of a hoof on a horse-track—
　　　　A horse-riding horse for a horse track—
　　　　Conifer county of Surrey approached
　　Through remarkable wrought-iron gates.

Over your boundary now, I wash my face in a bird-bath,
　　Then which path shall I take? that over there by the pram?
Down by the pond! —yes, I will take the slippery third path,
　　　　Trodden away with gym shoes,
　　　　Beautiful fir-dry alley that leads
　　To the beautiful body of Pam.

Pam, I adore you, Pam, you great big mountainous sports girl,
　　Whizzing them over the net, full of the strength of five:
That old Malvernian brother, you zephyr and khaki shorts girl,
　　　　Although he's playing for Woking,
　　　　Can't stand up
　　To your wonderful backhand drive.

See the strength of her arm, as firm and hairy as Hendren's:
　　See the size of her thighs, the pout of her lips as, cross,
And full of a pent-up strength, she swipes at the rhododendrons,

Lucky the rhododendrons,
And flings her arrogant love-lock
Back with a petulant toss.

Over the redolent pinewoods, in at the bathroom casement,
One fine Saturday, Windelsham bells shall call:
Up the Butterfield aisle rich with Gothic enlacement,
Licensed now for embracement,
Pam and I, as the organ
Thunders over you all.

I don't like any of my verses very much; only the one I am engaged on at the time interests me.

I can see a certain skill in rhythm and use of words in "Pot-Pourri from a Surrey Garden," as the verses, like all my verse, are meant to be recited out loud. The verses too imply the semirural landscape of Surrey where strong girls play tennis and strong sons go to the right class of school for children of canasta-playing parents who live in half-timbered well-appointed villas among the conifers.

The impression I wanted to convey was of unbountiful and littered country with Victorian churches built in areas developed when the railways came out to those parts at the end of the last century, to bring commuters from the City.

Simple sex and unquestioning Faith in things as they are and the idea that God's in his heaven all's right with the world are, I suppose, the underlying themes. Anyhow, the poem is unpretentious and less morbid than is usually so.

William Empson

BACCHUS

The laughing god born of a startling answer
    (Cymbal of clash in the divided glancer
    Forcing from heaven's the force of earth's desire)
Capped a retort to sublime earth by fire
And starred round within man its salt and glitter
    (Round goblet, but for star- or whirled- map fitter?
    Earth lost in him is still but earth fulfilled),
Troubled the water till the spirit 'stilled
And flowered round tears-of-wine round the dimmed flask
    (The roundest ones crack least under this task;
    It is the delicate glass stands heat, better than stone.
    This is the vessel could have stood alone
    Were it not fitted both to earth and sky),
Which trickled to a sea, though wit was dry,
Making a brew thicker than blood, being brine,
Being the mother water which was first made blood,
All living blood, and whatever blood makes wine.

The god arkitect whose coping with the Flood
Groyned the white stallion arches of the main
    (And miner deeps that in the dome of the brain
    Take Iris' arches' pupillage and Word)
Walked on the bucking water like a bird
And, guard, went round its rampart and its ball
    (Columbus' egg sat on earth's garden wall

And held the equitation of his bar;
    Waves beat his bounds until he foamed a star
    And mapped with fire the skyline that he ploughed),
Trod and divined the inwheeling serene cloud,
    (And who knows if Narcissus dumb and bent—)
Shed and fermented to a firmament
    (—May use his pool as mirror for the skies?)
Blind Hera's revelation peacock eyes
    (Before-and-behind
    Trophies the golden throne
    May still be planted on;
    Incestuous Chaos will breed permanent).
Helled to earth's centre Ixion at the wheel
    (He boxed the compassing of his appeal.
    Her centaur, born thence, schooled
    This hero, the paunched beaker, ether-cooled)
Still makes go round the whirled fooled clouded wheal.

The god who fled down with a standard yard
    (Surveying with that reed which was his guard
    He showed to John the new Jerusalem.
    It was a sugar-cane containing rum,
    And hence the fire on which these works depend)
Taught and quivered strung upon the bend
An outmost crystal a recumbent flame
    (He drinks all cups the tyrant could acclaim;
    He still is dumb, illimitably wined;
    Burns still his nose and liver for mankind . . .)
It is an ether, such an agony.
In the thin choking air of Caucasus
He under operation lies for ever

Smelling the chlorine in the chloroform.
The plains around him flood with the destroyers
Pasturing the stallions in the standing corn.

The herm whose length measured degrees of heat
    (Small lar that sunned itself in Mercury
      And perked one word there that made space ends meet)
Fluttered his snake too lightly in to see
    (Most fertile thief, and journal to inquire)
The mortal Eden forming, and the fire.
A smash resounding in its constancy.
This burst the planet Bacchus in the sky.
Thence dry lone asteroids took heart to be.
So soon the amalgam with mercury
This plumbing: given with it free, the house
Not built with hands: the silver crucible,
Butt-armed: the sovereigns: eats into flaked sloughs.
Paste for the backs of mirrors, there he lies;
Leper scales fall always from his eyes.

She whom the god had snatched into a cloud
Came up my stair and called to me across
The gulf she floated over of despair.
Came roaring up as through triumphal arches
Called I should warm my hands on her gold cope
Called her despair the coping of her fire.

The god in making fire from her despair
Cast from the parabola of falling arches
An arch that cast his focus to the skyline
    Cold focus burning from the other's fire

Arachne sailing her own rope of cloud
    A Tracer photon with a rocket's life-line
And purged his path with a thin fan of fire.

Round steel behind the lights of the god's car

A wheel of fire that span her head across
Borne soaring forward through a crowd of cloud
Robed in fire round as heaven's cope
The god had lit up her despair to fire
Fire behind grates of a part of her despair
And rang like bells the vaults and the dark arches.

I am afraid I like *Bacchus* best of my own poems, maybe as the traditional mother dotes on the imbecile. Dylan Thomas approved of it more than my other poems too. It may seem to the put-upon reader who works at it (of course it is not meant to be just Imagist) a very intellectual box of tricks, also rather put together at random; but if that were all it couldn't have been so hard to finish. I failed for years to do the central verse, about Prometheus, and then in 1939 I was invited on a little shooting trip in Northern Indo-China during the holidays. On the first evening of the drive out, after a certain amount of celebration, I fell into some pit and dislocated my arm. We were in reach of a French doctor, who gave me gas to put it back; and he said he had never seen a man coming out of gas looking so pleased. Exalted rather was what I was; I had discovered triumphantly that something *was* something else, and it was quite incidental that I had seen what to write in the poem. But I asked for a pencil as soon as I had collected myself, and still had till recently the bit of paper with

Pasturing the stallions in the standing corn

scrawled on it with my left hand.

However, though I feel that this somehow proves the poem is genuine, the idea wasn't at all hard to come by; we refugees from the Japanese were regularly hearing that they had turned their hordes into the ricefields. Maybe a lot of ideas which we accept without surprise were arrived at by an illumination.

Critics have often said that my earlier poetry was tolerably close to the rhythms of the spoken language, whereas I ended in the dead rhetoric of the end-stopped ten-syllable line. But if you are trying to be vatic it is natural to be end-stopped and uncolloquial, and to say that a poem mustn't be vatic is doctrinaire; even though I have against me the strong and improbable combination of Dr. Leavis and Professor Robert Graves. Even this poem, I think, can be read so that the excitement piles up; but I wouldn't deny that it is a tiresome genre, and not what a writer should go on repeating.

William Empson

Richmond Lattimore

ANNIVERSARY

Where were we in that afternoon? And where
is the high room now, the bed on which you laid your hair,
as bells beat early in the still air?

A two o'clock of sun and shutters. Oh, recall
the chair's angle a stripe of shadow on the wall,
the hours we gathered in our hands, and then let fall.

Wrist on wrist we relive memory, shell of moon
on day-sky, two o'clock in lazy June,
and twenty years gone in an afternoon.

There were several poems I might have chosen which say more
and about which more could be said, but I would as soon be repre-
sented by a straight lyric, best perhaps because shortest, as by any-
thing else.

The place is Athens. Several changes were made after the first
draft. The most important is where "Finger on red pulse relives
memory" was changed to "Wrist on wrist we relive memory."

It is hard to analyze something I have written and chosen without
self-praise. Looking at it as if someone else had written it, I would
say that, within the general rhetorical framework, the decisive stroke
is the phrase "shell of moon/on day-sky."

Richmond Lattimore

Vernon Watkins

POET AND GOLDSMITH

He was now alone. The lovers had wandered across
The field. About him the air fell sweet with singing.
Very close to his eyes a bird was carrying moss.
It gathered a wisp of straw, pecked, and looked up,
And flew to a secret nest. He watched the bough
Tremble. Now it was still. There was dew on the field.
Petals began to close. The roots of the elms
Held his wonder: 'Be warned: about you are symbols.'

Over sea, gold distance hung in a fiery crucible.
No fingers, however cunning, could sift the grains
Of hurrying sand. Mathematical, yet inscrutable,
Each rose with the rising wave, then slipped through the hour-
    glass.
No shore could set a term to the curlew's call.
The voice returned to itself round the sevenfold world
And perched on mystery. Night, like a working goldsmith,
Heard waves beat on the industructible core.

The poet sang: 'All ages bud like the sycamore.
Brown keys spin down to beginning. There are two natures.
Blest are the lost, packed hidden within life's door
Like seeds in the husk. Yet, since a small man climbed
The crooked trunk, and groped, and sat in the branch,
The minutiae of earth are changed, and the blackbird's praises

Are now twofold: they speak, and they speak beyond
   knowledge.
Even so, these hands have touched the harp of the dead.'

The dying light moved down to birth in his eyes,
And his eyes experienced music. Night was athletic;
A powerful glory tensed the proportioned skies.
And he murmured again: 'One thought that is dear to love:
True characters do not age in each other's eyes.
Indeed, we die each moment the life of another,
And there is no separation, no spear in the side,
Except in that forgetting of mutual death.'

'Unsearchable distance! The gliding avalanche
Wounds me,' he sang. Sycamore leaves against heaven
Moving, sighed. Then, as he touched one branch,
The force of his fingers entered the roots of the tree.
'Earth, cradle of riches; the speed and grace of the hunter,
Born here; plumes of the pheasant shining with dew:
They speak, singly, of inexhaustible treasure.
Night speaks, the artificer, beating out gold.'

I cannot pick a single poem to represent me better than others,
so I pick one that is near the root of everything I write. It is from
my book *Cypress and Acacia*, published early in 1960. This poem,
with its very slight element of rhyme, is built upon the pivotal point
between one way of writing and another. It is about nature, and
about transfigured nature. To those who have never looked through
or beyond nature, if there are such people, it must be meaningless.
Unredeemed nature can only offer to the poet a vista which leads

to despair, and it is the liberation from that despair which is the motif of this poem and the substance of its exultation.

The very last words of the poem came to me many years before the poem was made, but when I began to write it, nine or ten years later, I used the provisional title "Taliesin at Sunset." Taliesin was an early Welsh poet who claimed to have lived in all ages. I changed the title, and I am glad I changed it, but the elements of the first title are there. You may, if you like, say that this poem is about Taliesin looking at the created universe from the standpoint of Christian faith, which I call the pivotal point between one way of writing and another.

Vernon Watkins

Paul Engle

BEASTS

I
That was a shocking day
When we watched, lying prone,
The two trout sidle under
The underwater stone;

When we saw there beyond
The hedge of hardy thorn
The eager touch of summer
Luring the lifted corn;

When down the slope the two
Running red fox dared
Daylight in their need,
Poised, aloof and paired;

When cardinals from green
Willows, with red cries,
Scarlet scream of bird,
Plunged in our pool of eyes;

For we, merely woman
And man, did not believe
Living things could love
Wholly, and not grieve;

For love had always been
A nimble animal
That could lure innocence
Or lewd on its belly crawl;

By snarl, by sensual cry,
Love lived, but in a cage,
Barred by my own tight pride
And your rehearsed pure rage;

Pride, pride that would not let
Self give up utterly,
Rage, rage that self *would* give
Itself up utterly.

They leapt at us like fire
And burned us with our blame,
Defied us with delight,
And shamed our human shame.

II
We have seen animals,
Finned, furred and feathered, move
From their straight courses, curve
Into one line of love:

Fish, fox and cardinal,
Unreasoning and quick,
Proved one and one are one
By plain arithmetic.

They shocked us with their proof:
Those pairs of parallel
Loves that met and merged
Our own fused futures tell:

Each in the other's view—
Two lines of living light—
Will bend through the bent eye
One ecstacy of sight.

Our shattered parallels
Of rigid rage and pride
Will bend in one live length
Closer than side by side.

This is a favorite poem because it makes an effort to mimic its intensity of feeling with an intensity of form. The poem says that the animals which it describes "Proved one and one are one/By plain arithmetic." So the writing also tries to become one with the felt idea which it tries to express.

Love is a triumph over all obstacles, including opposites. The stanzas make their own attempt to triumph over artificiality of rime, meter and formal rhythm, by making strong and spontaneous emotion not only survive these hazards, but in a sense depend on them. Thus the notion of opposites is not only the theme of the poem, but also its manner.

The poem was a trouble to write, but also a pleasure. It was a temptation not to give in too much to the playing on words, and yet in some stanzas that same lightness was crucial to the meaning: "Defied us with delight/And shamed our human shame."

One of the allurements in the writing was the contrast between the two sections, also a part of the concept of opposites. The first section moves more rapidly, is more precise, more concrete, more physical, more sensual. The second is more deliberate, more general, more abstract (wicked word). This is the sort of thing which fascinates the poet, often to his great distress, to his great distraction.

The first section offers a statement, the second section offers a mathematical restatement of the same idea. The first section offers proof that love can merge two people; the second offers a prophecy that it will. This working of plain details on one hand (the fish, the corn) with generalization on the other is also a part of the opposites in resolution which the poem attempts to prove.

I also have a fondness for the poem because it came with a longer group of poems, all of them variations on the theme of love, published as a book, *The Word of Love*. Looking at it again, I remember the compulsion of working every evening of a spring season in Louisiana (Baton Rouge) when the urgent emotion demanded that language be put under control.

All of the above sounds too cold-blooded. I hope that the poem defies the explanation.

Paul Engle

Theodore Roethke

WORDS FOR THE WIND

I
Love, love, a lily's my care,
She's sweeter than a tree.
Loving, I use the air
Most lovingly: I breathe;
Mad in the wind I wear
Myself as I should be,
All's even with the odd,
My brother the vine is glad.

Are flower and seed the same?
What do the great dead say?
Sweet Phoebe, she's my theme:
She sways whenever I sway.
"O love me while I am,
You green thing in my way!"
I cried, and the birds came down
And made my song their own.

Motion can keep me still:
She kissed me out of thought
As a lovely substance will;
She wandered; I did not:

I stayed, and light fell
Across her pulsing throat;
I stared, and a garden stone
Slowly became the moon.

The shallow stream runs slack;
The wind creaks slowly by;
Out of a nestling's beak
Comes a tremulous cry
I cannot answer back;
A shape from deep in the eye—
That woman I saw in a stone—
Keeps pace when I walk alone.

II
The sun declares the earth;
The stones leap in the stream;
On a wide plain, beyond
The far stretch of a dream,
A field breaks like the sea;
The wind's white with her name,
And I walk with the wind.

The dove's my will today.
She sways, half in the sun:
Rose, easy on a stem,
One with the sighing vine,
One to be merry with,
And pleased to meet the moon.
She likes wherever I am.

Passion's enough to give
Shape to a random joy:
I cry delight: I know
The root, the core of a cry.
Swan-heart, arbutus-calm,
She moves when time is shy:
Love has a thing to do.

A fair thing grows more fair;
The green, the springing green
Makes an intenser day
Under the rising moon;
I smile, no mineral man;
I bear, but not alone,
The burden of this joy.

III
Under a southern wind,
The birds and fishes move
North, in a single stream;
The sharp stars swing around;
I get a step beyond
The wind, and there I am,
I'm odd and full of love.

Wisdom, where is it found?—
Those who embrace, believe.
Whatever was, still is,
Says a song tied to a tree.
Below, on the ferny ground,
In rivery air, at ease,
I walk with my true love.

What time's my heart? I care.
I cherish what I have
Had of the temporal:
I am no longer young
But the winds and waters are;
What falls away will fall;
All things bring me to love.

IV
The breath of a long root,
The shy perimeter
Of the unfolding rose,
The green, the altered leaf,
The oyster's weeping foot,
And the incipient star—
Are part of what she is.
She wakes the ends of life.

Being myself, I sing
The soul's immediate joy.
Light, light, where's my repose?
A wind wreathes round a tree.
A thing is done: a thing
Body and spirit know
When I do what she does:
Creaturely creature, she!—

I kiss her moving mouth,
Her swart hilarious skin;
She breaks my breath in half;
She frolics like a beast;
And I dance round and round,

A fond and foolish man,
And see and suffer myself
In another being, at last.

Allow me a purely personal choice: "Words for the Wind."

For those who are interested in such matters: the poem is an epithalamion to a bride seventeen years younger. W. H. Auden had given us his house, in Forio, Ischia, for several months, as a wedding present. It was my first trip to Europe. A real provincial, I was frightened by Italy, but within a few days, the sun, the Mediterranean, the serenity of the house changed everything. I was able to move outside myself—for me sometimes a violent dislocation—and express a joy in another, in others: I mean Beatrice O'Connell, and the Italian people, their world, their Mediterranean.

The piece is written in a line-length that interested me from the beginning ("Open House," "The Adamant," and the like). But here the beat is a good deal swifter, the rhythms more complex. I would like to think, of course, that something other than the usual has been effected in an old form.

Theodore Roethke

Stephen Spender

THE GENEROUS YEARS

(Aetat 18)

His are the generous days that balance
Soul and body. Should he hear the trumpet
Behind the sun that sends its thinning ray
Penetrating to the marrow—
At once one with that cause, he'd throw
Himself across some high far parapet,
Body die to soul down the sheer way
Of consummation in the summons.

His also are the days when should he greet
Her who goes walking, looking for a brooch
Under broad leaves at dusk beside the path
—And sidelong looks at him as though she thought
His smile might hide the gleam she sought—
He would run up to her and each
Find the lost clasp hid in them both,
Soul live to body where they meet.

Body soul, soul body, seem one breath,
Or the twined shadows of the sun, his will,
In these his generous days, to prove
His own true nature only is to give.

Wholly to die, or wholly else to live!
Body to soul, and let the bright cause kill,
Or soul to body, let the blood make love.
Giving is death in life and life in death.

After, of course, will come a time not this
When he'll be taken, stripped, strapped to a wheel
That is a world, and has the power to change
The brooch's gold, the trumpet scarlet blaze
—The lightning in the bones those generous days—
Into what drives a system, like a fuel.
Then to himself he will seem loathed and strange
Have thoughts yet colder than the thing he is.

"The Generous Years" is one of my favorites because it sums up those feelings I have had for about twenty-five years, since the time of the Spanish Civil War, about those who might have lived but who chose to die.

It is also a poem which I have taken exceptional pains over (I must have written at least 100 attempts at it), and that, of course, attaches one to a poem.

Stephen Spender

Elizabeth Bishop

THE MAN-MOTH*

Here, above,
cracks in the buildings are filled with battered moonlight.
The whole shadow of Man is only as big as his hat.
It lies at his feet like a circle for a doll to stand on,
and he makes an inverted pin, the point magnetized to the
    moon.
He does not see the moon; he observes only her vast
    properties,
feeling the queer light on his hands, neither warm nor cold,
of a temperature impossible to record in thermometers.

But when the Man-Moth
pays his rare, although occasional, visits to the surface,
the moon looks rather different to him. He emerges
from an opening under the edge of one of the sidewalks
and nervously begins to scale the faces of the buildings.
He thinks the moon is a small hole at the top of the sky,
proving the sky quite useless for protection.
He trembles, but must investigate as high as he can climb.

Up the facades,
his shadow dragging like a photographer's cloth behind him,
he climbs fearfully, thinking that this time he will manage

* Newspaper misprint for "mammoth."

to push his small head through that round clean opening
and be forced through, as from a tube, in black scrolls on the
   light.
(Man, standing below him, has no such illusions.)
But what the Man-Moth fears most he must do, although
he fails, of course, and falls back scared but quite unhurt.

             Then he returns
to the pale subways of cement he calls his home. He flits,
he flutters, and cannot get aboard the silent trains
fast enough to suit him. The doors close swiftly.
The Man-Moth always seats himself facing the wrong way
and the train starts at once at its full, terrible speed,
without a shift in gears or a gradation of any sort.
He cannot tell the rate at which he travels backwards.

             Each night he must
be carried through artificial tunnels and dream recurrent
   dreams.
Just as the ties recur beneath his train, these underlie
his rushing brain. He does not dare look out the window,
for the third rail, the unbroken draught of poison,
runs there beside him. He regards it as a disease
he has inherited the susceptibility to. He has to keep
his hands in his pockets, as others must wear mufflers.

             If you catch him,
hold up a flashlight to his eye. It's all dark pupil,
an entire night itself, whose haired horizon tightens
as he stares back, and closes up the eye. Then from the lids
one tear, his only possession, like the bee's sting, slips.

Slyly he palms it, and if you're not paying attention
he'll swallow it. However, if you watch, he'll hand it over,
cool as from underground springs and pure enough to drink.

This poem was written in 1935 when I first lived in New York City.

I've forgotten what it was that was supposed to be "mammoth." But the misprint seemed meant for me. An oracle spoke from the page of the *New York Times*, kindly explaining New York City to me, at least for a moment.

One is offered such oracular statements all the time, but often misses them, gets lazy about writing them out in detail, or the meaning refuses to stay put. This poem seems to me to have stayed put fairly well—but as Fats Waller used to say, "One never knows, do one?"

Elizabeth Bishop

J. V. Cunningham

EPITAPH

When I shall be without regret
And shall mortality forget,
When I shall die who lived for this,
I shall not miss the things I miss.
And you who notice where I lie
Ask not my name. It is not I.

I like this poem because it is all denotation and no connotation; because it has only one level of meaning; because it is not ironic, paradoxical, complex, or subtle; and because the meter is monotonously regular.

J. V. Cunningham

Josephine Miles

REASON

Said, Pull her up a bit will you, Mac, I want to unload there.
Said, Pull her up my rear end, first come first serve.
Said, Give her the gun, Bud, he needs a taste of his own
    bumper.
Then the usher came out and got into the act:

Said, Pull her up, pull her up a bit, we need this space, sir.
Said, For God's sake, is this still a free country or what?
You go back and take care of Gary Cooper's horse
And leave me handle my own car.

Saw them unloading the lame old lady,
Ducked out under the wheel and gave her an elbow,
Said, All you needed to do was just explain;
Reason, Reason is my middle name.

"Reason" is a favorite one of my poems because I like the idea of
speech—not images, not ideas, not music, but people talking—as the
material from which poetry is made. So much inert surface, so many
hidden depths, such systematic richness of play in tone and color,
with these I too easily become impatient in modern poetry, because
I like the spare and active interplay of talk.

Like the young man from Japan, I like to get as many unimportant syllables in a five-stress line as I possibly can. Then they can't be implicative.

And the accents of a limited and maybe slightly misplaced pride interest me. Good strong true pride we need more of, and oblique accents of it at least sound out the right direction.

Josephine Miles

Kenneth Patchen

THE LITTLE GREEN BLACKBIRD

I

BECAUSE *the ground-creature looked so sad*
The little green blackbird watched a sunflower
And a child's swing and an old woman crying.
So the tiger asked him if he'd seen
The little green blackbird around anywhere.
The tiger was there too, and also
A tiger just in from the forest.
Well, the little green blackbird also watched
A willow tree's birth and a winged crocodile too.
So then the lion asked him if he'd seen
The little green blackbird around anywhere.
You see, the lion was there too, and also
A huge bearded mouse that looked like a lion,
But was really a fat brown fish too lazy to shave;
In those days, only the most timid barbers took along
Their razors when they went in swimming.
But the little green blackbird felt pretty good
And he got himself a cuckoo named Willie Watt,
A baby whale named Willie Watt, and a big yeller hound dog
Which everyone called Willie Watt, but whose name
Was really Willie Watt; in those days, nobody minded.
So the flea's sister asked him if he'd seen
The little green blackbird around anywhere.
The flea's wife was there too, and also
An uncle of the flea's cousin's sister,
Who was also Willie Watt's father. You see, in those days,
Nobody minded and it was pretty nice.

II

BECAUSE *the boy-headed lark played one*
The little green blackbird became quite anxious
To try the little-known guitar-trombone-ophone
For himself; however, before having a go at it,
He went up into the Great Smoky Mountains
And there meditated eleven years with nothing
To eat or drink except a variety of foods
And beverages. Then, one evening toward night,
It suddenly came to him to wonder
Why the sky was up above there; and also,
Whether, if he could stand on top of it,
The sky might not wonder the same thing about him.
So he ran lickity-split down the mountain
And told an old fellow on a bike about
His idea: (Of course at the time he didn't know
That the bulgy-legged old fellow was a train robber,
But when he got home his was gone . . . and only a few
Wisps of stale steam still clung round the cabin door.)
"Alas," said the little green blackbird sadly;
"I always thought it just another futility of speech,
That 'train of thought' thing. Oh well, I'll drop by
The Nightingale Café; perhaps Dolly and Kate and the Captain
Will be back from their wedding. Now, let me see . . .
'Accumulation' is a long word; and 'candles'
Is another, though its length is more variable."

III

BECAUSE *his sister saw Shakespeare in the moon*
The little green blackbird decided to study
Some history and geography; now, this meant going
To places like Portugal and Ayr Moor Gullibaad;
So he had some cards printed and

Handed them out. This of course started
A war, because the cards were printed
With ink. And the little green blackbird
Arrived in Portugal not only without cards,
But without a head, or arms, or legs,
Or even a little toe. This might not have been
So bad had he been feeling all right.
And it was no better in Ayr Moor Gullireet either;
In fact, it was just as sad really. "So much
For history and geography," he reflected
Ruefully; "but at least I'm a lot luckier
Than those poor unfortunates who still have heads
Left to think about what's going to happen to them."

IV

BECAUSE *he kept imagining a pensive rabbit*
The little green blackbird went off outdoors
And sat on a tree under a spreading chair.
When the sun came out it got dark
But the little green blackbird hadn't ever
Felt that lonely before and he laughed.
So some dinnerplates broke, the sun awoke,
The waitress in her flowered apron spoke;
And the little green blackbird sadly answered:
"If a friend of mine comes inquiring for me,
Tell him I've gone to join my grief
To the wintry crying of the northern sea."
And he leaned back with a puzzled smile,
Like the tiger amused by a sundial.
So the door closed, the rain closed,
The sun closed; also, the moon, a jar
Of raisin pudding, the tenth of January,
And half a raccoon. Now, alas, there was

Nothing left except the world; and nobody
In his right mind expects the world
To do anything now except close.

V

BECAUSE *his friend claimed there weren't any*
The little green blackbird ran on and on
Until he chanced to meet a little green blackbird.
But the little green blackbird couldn't get
His car to work and so he said,
"Will you come to my house at seven?
Mike and Ellie are there right now;
However, if they don't show up, Joe Bill
Has promised to rub fresh mud into
Our shirts over behind the new schoolhouse."
"And what will that cost us?" asked
The little green blackbird, adjusting his thumbs.
"Only fifty apiece," answered the little green blackbird.
"Besides, I'm not so sure I like your attitude!
Obviously you're drunk. Here, help me up."
So the little green blackbird drove off
Down the road until he reached a bridge;
Then, adjusting his cap, and his thumbs,
He said, "What are you doing in that river?"
And the little green blackbird replied sharply,
"Waiting for Joe Bill's sister, that's what!
She comes here every Tuesday to wash his shirt."
"But this is Tuesday," the little green blackbird
Snorted, pausing to adjust his parade hat,
His honey-bee-striped hip-length socks,
His bright red paper wading boots, and
His well-worn thumbs: "You must be drunker
Than I thought!" And he drove into the lake.

VI

BECAUSE *it's good to keep things straight*
Now the little green blackbird liked a mouse
And a Malayan sunbear and a horse
And a beetle and a mouse and a horse
And a mouse and a leopard and a beaver
And a black fox and a fox squirrel and a lion
And a buffalo and a beaver and a donkey
And a tiger and a gorilla and a panther
And a salamander and a periwinkle and an ox
And an elephant and an alligator and an armadillo
And a mouse and a mule and a beetle
And a moonfish and a buffalo and a snail
And a horse and a lion and a butterfly
And a horse and a tiger and a mouse;
And the leopard and the donkey and the horse
And the buffalo and the ox and the elephant
And the mouse and the beetle and the gorilla
And the horse and the periwinkle and the mouse
And the panther and the lion and the tiger
And the butterfly and the beaver and the snail
Also liked the little green blackbird;
But the horse and the armadillo and the lion
And the buffalo were quite indifferent to him;
While the beetle and the mouse and the moonfish
And the salamander and the mule and the beaver
Didn't care one way or the other about him;
Whereas the mouse and the horse and the mouse
And the tiger didn't even know he existed.

VII

BECAUSE *growing a mustache was pretty tiring*
The little green blackbird's father always said:
"A bear and a bean and a bee in bed,
Only on Bogoslof Island can one still get
That good old-fashioned white brown bread!" This made a
Very deep impression on the little green blackbird,
So he decided to forget the whole thing.
But first he painted a stolen motorcycle on the sidewalk
And sold it to a nearsighted policeman.
By then of course the little green blackbird
Remembered that his father also did impressions
Of J. Greenstripe Whittier on freshly-painted parkbenches.
So he invited nineteen hundred rabbits over for dinner;
And they each brought him a tin-plated goldfish,
A handful of gloves, the drawing of a frosty breath,
And one of those decks of newfangled playing cards,
The kind that bite people. Well, when it came time
To go home, all nineteen thousand rabbits filed out
In a pregnant silence, that was broken only
By the sound of their low-pitched voices
Raised in speech. Whereupon the father
Of the little green blackbird quietly said:
"It is our sentence, to endure;
And our only crime, that we are here to serve it."

I like TLGBb best because of all my pieces it's the only one I've ever made such a ridiculous statement about. So the special attention . . .

Kenneth Patchen

Roy Fuller

THE IDES OF MARCH

Fireballs and thunder augment the wailing wind:
A vulgar score, but not inappropriate
To my romantic, classic situation.
Within the house my wife is asleep and dreaming
That I, too, am cocooned inside the world
Of love whose fear is that the other world
Will end it. But I wait uneasy here
Under the creaking trees, the low dark sky,
For the conspirators. This is the place
Where I come, in better weather, with a book
Or pen and paper—for I must confess
To a little amateur scribbling. Love and letters:
One ought to be content—would, if the times
Were different; if state and man were free,
The slaves fed well, and wars hung over us
Not with death's certainty but with the odds
Merely of dying a not too painful death.
Yes, I have caught the times like a disease
Whose remedy is still experimental;
And felt the times as some enormous gaffe
I cannot forget. And now I am about
To cease being a fellow traveller, about
To select from several complex panaceas,
Like a shy man confronted with a box
Of chocolates, the plainest after all.

I am aware that in my conscious wish
To rid the empire of a tyrant there
Is something that will give me personal pleasure;
That usually one's father's death occurs
About the time one becomes oneself a father.
These subtleties are not, I think, important—
No more than that I shall become a traitor,
Technically, to my class, my friend, my country.
No, the important thing is to remove
Guilt from this orchard, which is why I have
Invited here those men of action with
Their simpler motives and their naked knives.
I hope my wife will walk out of the house
While I am in their compromising presence,
And know that what we built had no foundation
Other than luck and my false privileged role
In a society that I despised.
And then society itself, aghast,
Reeling against the statue also will
Be shocked to think I had a secret passion.
Though passion is, of course, not quite the word:
I merely choose what history foretells.
The dawn comes moonlike now between the trees
And silhouettes some rather muffled figures.
It is embarrassing to find oneself
Involved in this clumsy masquerade. There still
Is time to send a servant with a message:
'Brutus is not at home'; time to postpone
Relief and fear. Yet, plucking nervously
The pregnant twigs, I stay. Good morning, comrades.

Difficult for me and I suppose for most poets to pick a single poem to represent them. In my case I sometimes think that my better poems are aside rather from what over the years have been my poetic "aims," or consist of a sequence too long to reproduce here, like my "Mythological Sonnets" or "Faustian Sketches." The poem I have chosen, "The Ides of March," suffers, too, in my eyes, from being in blank verse, because the search for rhymes has always helped to loosen up my rather too rational and logical attitude to the composition of poetry. But in this poem, which was written in 1954, I think I found a good "objective correlative" for a theme that has bothered me since I started to write verse in the early thirties. That theme is, simply, the relationship between the intellectual and the world of affairs. In my poetic youth the poems of Wilfred Owen were rediscovered, with their preface exhorting true poets to be truthful and to warn society about dangers only poets could detect. The new poets of the day, Auden, Spender, Day Lewis, carried these precepts into effect by writing about the evils of the Depression and the necessity for the creation of a juster society. But there is an obvious contradiction between the private pleasures of writing poetry and the discomfort of political action; between the sheltered origin and life of the artist and the sufferings of the unemployed or the Jew; between the sophisticated search for truth of the intellectual and the crudities of political belief. The poet tends to oscillate between the extremes of giving up poetry for action (e.g. going off to fight in the Spanish Civil War) and writing off as quite unsuitable for poets all action other than the act of composition. By the time I wrote "The Ides of March" I was able to be a bit detached and ironical about this theme. For one thing, the mere business of growing older made political problems seem less vital and less personal. For another, I had had a few years of "action" of a kind by serving in the Royal Navy during the War, and no doubt felt that this absolved me from some of the guilt of being an inactive artist. So my Brutus has few illusions about the conspirators he is going to join. Again, by alluding to the legend that Brutus was Caesar's natural son, I enabled myself to give the hero of my poem some psychoanalytical insight into his situation. Finally, the "dramatic monologue" form of the poem, and the assumption of the persona and locale of Act II, Scene 1, of Shakespeare's play, permitted me to escape from the tyranny of the first person singular which I think has governed my poetry too much. The book in which the poem appeared, *Brutus's Orchard*, (the title clearly indicated an area of tension categorizing the collection as a whole) contained a few other poems in which the poet assumed a mask, and in my work since then the mask has been predominant. To be "truthful" the poet need not speak *in propria persona* and society can be warned in quite fictitious terms—these are the modest principles that were perhaps first announced in my verse by "The Ides of March." No doubt for many they are truisms, but for me, who was brought up puritanically in times of special crisis, they have changed my poetry's direction a little. Since 1950 I have written a number of novels: there, as well as with imagery and theme, one is, of course, concerned with character and plot. I like to think that these latter have also become, to some extent, the concerns of my verse.

Roy Fuller

Irving Layton

A TALL MAN EXECUTES A JIG

I

So the man spread his blanket on the field
And watched the shafts of light between the tufts
And felt the sun push the grass towards him;
The noise he heard was that of whizzing flies,
The whistlings of some small imprudent birds,
And the ambiguous rumbles of cars
That made him look up at the sky, aware
Of the gnats that tilted against the wind
And in the sunlight turned to jigging motes.
Fruitflies he'd call them except there was no fruit
About, spoiling to hatch these glitterings,
These nervous dots for which the mind supplied
The closing sentences from Thucydides,
Or from Euclid having a savage nightmare.

II

Jig jig, jig jig. Like minuscule black links
Of a chain played with by some playful
Unapparent hand or the palpitant
Summer haze bored with the hour's stillness.
He felt the sting and tingle afterwards
Of those leaving their orthodox unrest,
Leaving their undulant excitation
To drop upon his sleeveless arm. The grass,

Even the wildflowers became black hairs
And himself a maddened speck among them.
Still the assaults of the small flies made him
Glad at last, until he saw purest joy
In their frantic jiggings under a hair,
So changed from those in the unrestraining air.

III
He stood up and felt himself enormous.
Felt as might Donatello over stone,
Or Plato, or as a man who has held
A loved and lovely woman in his arms
And feels his forehead touch the emptied sky
Where all antinomies flood into light.
Yet jig jig jig, the haloing black jots
Meshed with the wheeling fire of the sun:
Motion without meaning, disquietude
Without sense or purpose, ephemerides
That mottled the resting summer air till
Gusts swept them from his sight like wisps of smoke.
Yet they returned, bringing a bee who, seeing
But a tall man, left him for a marigold.

IV
He doffed his aureole of gnats and moved
Out of the field as the sun sank down,
A dying god upon the blood-red hills.
Ambition, pride, the ecstasy of sex,
And all circumstance of delight and grief,
That blood upon the mountain's side, that flood
Washed into a clear incredible pool
Below the ruddied peaks that pierced the sun.
He stood still and waited. If ever

The hour of revelation was come
It was now, here on the transfigured steep.
The sky darkened. Some birds chirped. Nothing else.
He thought the dying god had gone to sleep:
An Indian fakir on his mat of nails.

V

And on the summit of the asphalt road
Which stretched towards the fiery town, the man
Saw one hill raised like a hairy arm, dark
With pines and cedars against the stricken sun
—The arm of Moses or of Joshua.
He dropped his head and let fall the halo
Of mountains, purpling and silent as time,
To see temptation coiled before his feet:
A violated grass-snake that lugged
Its intestine like a small red valise.
A cold-eyed skinflint it now was, and not
The manifest of that joyful wisdom,
The mirth and arrogant green flame of life;
Or earth's vivid tongue that flicked in praise of earth.

VI

And the man wept because pity was useless.
'Your jig's up; the flies come like kites,' he said
And watched the grass-snake crawl towards the hedge,
Convulsing and dragging into the dark
The satchel filled with curses for the earth,
For the odours of warm sedge, and the sun,
A blood-red organ in the dying sky.
Backwards it fell into a grassy ditch
Exposing its underside, white as milk,
And mocked by wisps of hay between its jaws;

And then it stiffened to its final length.
But though it opened its thin mouth to scream
A last silent scream that shook the black sky,
Adamant and fierce, the tall man did not curse.

VII

Beside the rigid snake the man stretched out
In fellowship of death; he lay silent
And stiff in the heavy grass with eyes shut,
Inhaling the moist odours of the night
Through which his mind tunnelled with flicking tongue
Backwards to caves, mounds, and sunken ledges
And desolate cliffs where come only kites,
And where of perished badgers and racoons
The claws alone remain, gripping the earth.
Meanwhile the green snake crept upon the sky,
Huge, his mailed coat glittering with stars that made
The night bright, and blowing thin wreaths of cloud
Athwart the moon; and as the weary man
Stood up, coiled above his head, transforming all.

Eschews the usual consolations, religious or poetic. No rhetorical huff-puff, no stertorous whine, so beloved by some of my contemporaries. Puts a gutted grass-snake at the centre of things and says to the lapis lazuli boys—"What's that you said about Art? Louder, the squirming creature can't hear you." Everything I ever knew about life and poetry, and some things that were revealed to me only at the last moment, has gone into its making. More than any other poem of mine, this one fuses feeling and thought in an intense moment of perception. Of truth. Truth for me, of course. That's the way I feel about gnats, and hills, and Christian renunciation, the pride of life and crushed grass-snakes writhing on the King's Highway. I like poems that are subtle and circular—the perfect form of a serpent swallowing its own tail and rolling towards Eternity. A meditative music, the feelings open as the sky. Formless poems give me the pips. If ideas, I want to see them dance. Otherwise it's historico-politico-economico uplift and braggadocio concealing a sad poverty of feeling. Worse, a poverty of imagination. The vulgar stance of the talentless mediocrity. The ambiguities of existence? Of course, of course. I think my poem reflects them, but NOT "Let's play Ambiguities, Empson and Brooks are watching, an ironical smile on their civilized faces." For all the big talk and big words and the big noises, only the genuine finally endures. The words that redeem us: justify the millions of slaughtered Xmas turkeys.

Irving Layton.

George Barker

EVENING STAR

Evening Star, enemy of lovers, why
Do you move so slowly across the sky
Now that another lover
Is warm under Maisie's bedcover?

I don't have any favourite poems, not even anyone else's, let alone
my own. (And I rather suspect this goes for a lot of poets—if there
are a lot of poets. It's as frivolous to have a favourite person—imag-
ine a menagerie full of *those* monsters.) So that in the circumstances
I would like to offer a little verse which I like for its simple sexual
irony. I also favour it because it is, I hope, opposite to much of the
pretentious pseudo-poetastry parading about public places now.

John Frederick Nims

THE NECROMANCERS

I

Clowns in a garish air. On panicky pedals
Managing monocycles for dear life.
And the heart pumps a ruby hoop—Fortuna's.
The princess flings our halo, knife by knife.

II

Tally the take in that affair with glory.
How I lay gaudy on the barbarous shore
Face burrowing in a patch of fern, blood stirring
Gamy as wines remembering summer stir.
No vein of all this flesh but leapt with memory:
Such splendor on lip and finger and the rest
As noon on a great range of sea, as heaven's
Moody amour, confusing east and west.

In grottos hung with cork and cordage bobbling
On halcyons where the lascar and his shade
Lay fecund in feluccas, heart atumble
Made love a plague of angels, raving, unmade.

Deep comas of the sun! My loafing shoulder
Ached for the sweetness pillared on your palm.
Ear to the ground heard dusky tambours: *coming.*
A crackle of skirt, sails bantering with calm.

The weight of sweetness then! I saw it settle
(Curled on a whirling skirt) in my dark dream.
And jubilant: *honey and sun, the blood!* Music
Demurred from the warm dark: *inhuman stream!*

A voice from long ago. And the warm darkness
Shuddered how often on the barbarous shore
Since two defied, palms conjuring, a bayou
The bitterns boom adieu, and guard no more.

The wheel that fractured light has come full-circle.
Leans with the poky spoke dust deepens on.
Ours sang and singing died. But all one summer
Who knew for sure that wonder from the sun?

III
Clowns in a garish air. On panicky pedals
Managing monocycles for dear life.
And the heart pumps a ruby hoop—Fortuna's.
The princess flings our halo, knife by knife.

When word-workers prefer this or that of their constructions, it may be because of what a more popular art would call the "real-life situation" of which they originated and to which, in the writer's memory, they have become the key—even though very little of that situation may have embodied itself in the work. Or it may be because of elements in the writing—perhaps merely of technique, of leger-demain—which have no real correspondence with anything that "hap-pened" outside the world of the poem. One might have the impres-sion that the composer of "The Necromancers" was interested in it for both reasons. The central section is concerned with memories of a summer spent by a southern ocean. The voice is that of a drowser, sun-drunk, love-drunk, lying face downward in the noonday heat, dreaming of the arrival of someone to whom his orientation is then deeply emotional. He imagines her coming up, resting her palm on his shoulder as she settles beside him. Then indeed she comes; and, his face still buried in the dark of his folded arm, he murmurs an interpretation of the moment—an interpretation she is moved to qualify. The reverie drifts off briefly into a mythical landscape, an Eden of portentous and affronted birds. From this it returns to a conclusion in terms of the sun-and-wheel imagery introduced earlier. A certain flourish, a certain exoticism and extravagance of language throughout may lead some to wonder if the writer's considered attitude to the experience is as single-minded as it seemed single-hearted. Parts I and III, added a year or more after the original composition, frame the experience—and thereby appraise it—in a context of circus imagery, of thrill and brilliance and comic desperation—the latter possibly mimed by the scrambling iambics of the first two lines, as more solemn effects are mimed by the pompous ionics ("on a great range," etc.) of the central section. The circus is a universal one: our blood, a precarious monocycle, spins around like the medieval wheel of fortune, rotating our careers to the same conclusion as that did. And meanwhile the knife-throwing carnival princess, who may or may not be the girl of the poem, is busily constructing our dazzling halo of danger.

John Frederick Nims

Delmore Schwartz

STARLIGHT LIKE INTUITION PIERCED THE TWELVE

The starlight's intuitions pierced the twelve,
The brittle night sky sparkled like a tune
Tinkled and tapped out on the xylophone.
Empty and vain, a glittering dune, the moon
Arose too big, and, in the mood which ruled,
Seemed like a useless beauty in a pit;
And then one said, after he carefully spat:
"No matter what we do, he looks at it!

"I cannot see a child or find a girl
Beyond his smile which glows like that spring moon."
"—Nothing no more the same," the second said,
"Though all may be forgiven, never quite healed
The wound I bear as witness, standing by;
No ceremony surely appropriate,
Nor secret love, escape or sleep because
No matter what I do, he looks at it—"

"Now," said the third, "no thing will be the same
I am as one who never shuts his eyes,
The sea and sky no more are marvellous,
And I no longer understand surprise!"

"Now," said the fourth, "nothing will be enough
—I heard his voice accomplishing all wit:
No word can be unsaid, no deed withdrawn
—No matter what is said, he measures it!"

"Vision, imagination, hope or dream,
Believed, denied, the scene we wished to see?
It does not matter in the least: for what
Is altered, if it is not true? That we
Saw goodness, as it is—*this* is the awe
And the abyss which we will not forget,
His story now the sky which holds all thought:
No matter what I think, think of it!"

"And I will never be what once I was,"
Said one for long as narrow as a knife,
"And we will never be what once we were;
We have died once; this is a second life."
"My mind is spilled in moral chaos," one
Righteous as Job exclaimed, "now infinite
Suspicion of my heart stems what I will
—No matter what I choose, he stares at it!"

"I am as one native in summer places
—Ten weeks' excitement paid for by the rich;
Debauched by that and then all winter bored,"
The sixth declared. "His peak left us a ditch!"
"He came to make this life more difficult,"
The seventh said, "No one will ever fit
His measure's heights, all is inadequate:
No matter what I do, what good is it?"

"He gave forgiveness to us: what a gift!"
The eighth chimed in. "But now we know how much
Must be forgiven. But if forgiven, what?
The crime which was will be; and the least touch
Revives the memory: what is forgiveness worth?"
The ninth spoke thus: "Who now will ever sit
At ease in Zion at the Easter feast?
No matter what the place, he touches it!"

"And I will always stammer, since he spoke,"
One, who had been most eloquent, said, stammering.
"I looked too long at the sun; like too much light,
So too much goodness is a boomerang,"
Laughed the eleventh of the troop. "I must
Try what he tried: I saw the infinite
Who walked the lake and raised the hopeless dead:
No matter what the feat, he first accomplished it!"

So spoke the twelfth; and then the twelve in chorus:
"Unspeakable unnatural goodness is
Risen and shines, and never will ignore us;
He glows forever in all consciousness;
Forgiveness, love, and hope possess the pit,
And bring our endless guilt, like shadow's bars:
No matter what we do, he stares at it!

What pity then deny? what debt defer?
We know he looks at us like all the stars,
And we shall never be as once we were,
This life will never be what once it was!"

"Starlight Like Intuition Pierced the Twelve" was written in 1943, and after so many years it is difficult for me to remember the reasons that caused the poem to be written with a spontaneity and delight which astonished me. But I do remember that for several years before, I had been reading the New Testament again and again, using a text with a very detailed Victorian commentary, and the text combined constantly with the commentary to make me think of modern poems I admired very much—particularly "Dover Beach," Hardy's "The Oxen," Valèry's "*Le Comitière Marin*," and Wallace Stevens' "Sunday Morning"—which were explicitly concerned with the decline of Christian belief or the impossibility of any belief whatever. So I think now that perhaps the chief reason the poem pleases me just as much as when I first wrote it is the way in which it dramatizes attitudes which accept Christianity as a reality while at the same time dismissing the question of literal belief as, at most, irrelevant. Thus stated, this is, I know, regarded as a recurrent doctrinal heresy by various Christian theologians. But the poem continues to give me a genuine emotional satisfaction partly despite and partly because of the literal claims of institutional Christianity.

Delmore Schwartz

Karl Shapiro

THE DIRTY WORD

The dirty word hops in the cage of the mind like the Pondi-cherry vulture, stomping with its heavy left claw on the sweet meat of the brain and tearing it with its vicious beak, ripping and chopping the flesh. Terrified, the small boy bears the big bird of the dirty word into the house, and grunting, puffing, carries it up the stairs to his own room in the skull. Bits of black feather cling to his clothes and his hair as he locks the staring creature in the dark closet.

All day the small boy returns to the closet to examine and feed the bird, to caress and kick the bird, that now snaps and flaps its wings savagely whenever the door is opened. How the boy trembles and delights at the sight of the white excre-ment of the bird! How the bird leaps and rushes against the walls of the skull, trying to escape from the zoo of the vocab-ulary! How wildly snaps the sweet meat of the brain in its rage.

And the bird outlives the man, being freed at the man's death-funeral by a word from the rabbi.

(But I one morning went upstairs and opened the door and entered the closet and found in the cage of my mind the great bird dead. Softly I wept it and softly removed it and softly buried the body of the bird in the hollyhock garden of the house I lived in twenty years before. And out of the worn black feathers of the wing have I made these pens to write these elegies, for I have outlived the bird, and I have mur-dered it in my early manhood.)

Why must grown people listen to rhymes? Why must meters be tapped out on nursery drums? Why hasn't America won the battle of Iambic Five? When are we going to grow up?

I wrote "The Dirty Word" almost twenty years ago and others in the same vein, yet it has taken me a lifetime to wear this form like my own coat. In those days I was just trying it on. Now I feel ashamed when I write meter and rhyme, or dirty, as if I were wearing a dress.

But this poem has always been my pride. St. John Perse admired it once and asked me why I wrote most of my things the other way. I told him it was hard to break a thousand-year-old habit. Now I am writing a whole book this way.

The dirty word is a kind of sacred mystery. That's what the poem is saying. It should not be used except with respect and intelligent fear. It should not be let out of the cage, as unfortunately it has been. It should not be domesticated. Nowadays the poor dirty word is dying of popcorn.

Karl Shapiro

John Berryman

THE DISPOSSESSED

'and something that . . that is theirs—no longer ours'
stammered to me the Italian page. A wood
seeded & towered suddenly. I understood.—

The Leading Man's especially, and the Juvenile Lead's,
and the Leading Lady's thigh that switches & warms,
and their grimaces, and their flying arms:

our arms, our story. Every seat was sold.
A crone met in a clearing sprouts a beard
and has a tirade. Not a word we heard.

Movement of stone within a woman's heart,
abrupt & dominant. They gesture how
fings really are. Rarely a child sings now

My harpsichord weird as a koto drums
adagio for twilight, for the storm-worn dove
no more de-iced, and the spidery business of love.

The Juvenile Lead's the Leader's arm, one arm
running the whole hole, branches, roots, (O watch)
and the faceless fellow waving from her crotch,

Stalin-unanimous! who procured a vote
and dare not use it, who have kept an eye
and dare not use it, percussive vote, clear eye.

That which a captain and a weaponeer
one day and one more day did, we did, *ach*
we did not, *They* did . . cam slid, the great lock

lodged, and no soul of us all was near was near,—
an evil sky (where the umbrella bloomed)
twirled its mustaches, hissed, the ingenue fumed,

poor virgin, and no hero rides. The race
is done. Drifts through, between the cold black trunks,
the peachblow glory of the perishing sun

in empty houses where old things take place.

Most writers are influenced either for or against various parts of
their work by the opinions admiring, hostile, or indifferent about
them that turn up from outside, and it may be that my (moderate)
liking for "The Dispossessed" is a product of the fact that only two
readers, so far as I know, have ever paid any attention to it: Jacques
Maritain who quoted it in one of his books and a critic (perhaps Mr.
Nims—I forget and haven't the issue at hand) who analyzed it at
some length in a *Poetry* Supplement when it first appeared. I don't
suggest, of course, that it is *worth* attention; I am only exploring
my own feeling. I think, though, that the liking is based rather on
my sense at the time of succeeding in some degree with a job I
set myself. This was 1947 or so. I was tired of writing noisy poems
like "New Year's Eve" and blowing poems like "Rock-study with

Wanderer"; I wanted something that would be both very neat, contained, and at the same time thoroughly mysterious.

I am not going to comment in detail on the poem, which is rather complicated. But it may be worth observing that I began with, or at any rate worked with, both the opposite directions the notion of dispossession points to: the miserable, *put out of one's own*, and the relieved, saved, un-devilled, de-spelled. The first is the more important, and the second need not be agreeable—the devil cast out may be life.

Particularly because I used the poem as title-piece for a book, I have been sensitive since (as indeed I was long before) to the word "dispossessed": and there can be no harm in saying here that I have come on it not dozens but hundreds of times used in the specially emphatic and central way I tried myself to achieve. The concept reaches deep into modern agony.

John Berryman

Barbara Howes

L'ILE DU LEVANT: THE NUDIST COLONY

All the wide air was trawled for cloud
And then that mass confined in a gray net
And moored to the horizon. Bowed

Down, the golden island under
A dull sky was not at its best; its heyday
Is when the heat crackles, the sun

Pours like a boiling waterfall
On matted underbrush and thicket, on
Boulder, dust; and, over all,

Cicadas at their pastime, drilling
Eyelets of sound, so many midget Singer
Sewing machines: busy, then still.

Landing beyond a thorny curve
We climbed down to the colony, extended
On its plot of beach. In the sudden swerve

Of every eye, they saw as one,
These Nudists on vacation, half their days
Prone, determined as chameleons

To match the ground beneath. At ease
Within a sandy cage, they turned to stare
Up at us clad identities

Who came to stare as openly
As if we too had railings fore and back
And the whole mind of a menagerie.

Such freedom of the flesh, if brave,
Lacks subtlety: a coat of sunburn can
Be badly cut. Well-tailored love

Not only demonstrates but hides,
Not only lodges with variety
But will keep private its dark bed.

We rose: below us golden-brown
Bodies of young and old, heavy and lean,
Lay beached upon the afternoon.

While water, casual as skin,
Bore our departing boat, we saw a form
In relief against the rocky line

And stood to wave farewell from our
World to his, even as charcoal dusk
Effaced his lazy semaphore.

It is difficult to know what to say in comment on this poem, or on why it was selected to join its fellows in this anthology. Perhaps it is suitable in being a companionable sort of work, neither unduly symbolic in conception nor strident in tone.

The island of Levant is located in the Mediterranean off the Côte d'Azur, within easy boating distance of Toulon and of St. Raphael to the east. In sight of its stony coast lie the more felicitous islands of Port-Cros and Porquerolles, which are adorned by beaches of the finest silvery sand, forests, and fishing hamlets whose restaurants serve up their bouillabaisse in great rectangular tureens of cork. This tree, which abounds on the mainland, forms a staple industry: a section of the rough bark is slashed and stripped off, and the tree is then left to recover and grow a new skin.

The vegetation on Levant, however, is mostly scrub, rough under-growth, stunted trees, and neither the Colony on the one half, nor the army installation on the other, has much to boast of in the way of natural beauty. All of this being true, it is surprising that the imagination did not first turn toward Porquerolles or Port-Cros for the subject for a poem. But that it did not, I suppose one must accept; one must accept its independent, even high-handed, ways. I can see that the beautiful sands of Porquerolles, over which a net-work of light plays down through clear water, must give precedence to the briars and cicadas of Levant. We must take it, I think, that the imagination has its reasons, and be prepared to follow the curious pathways it indicates.

Barbara Howes

Randall Jarrell

EIGHTH AIR FORCE

If, in an odd angle of the hutment
A puppy laps the water from a can
Of flowers, and the drunk sergeant shaving
Whistles *O Paradiso!*—shall I say that man
Is not as men have said: a wolf to man?

The other murderers troop in yawning;
Three of them play Pitch, one sleeps, and one
Lies counting missions, lies there sweating
Till even his heart beats: One; One; One.
O murderers! . . . Still, this is how it's done:

This is a war . . . But since these play, before they die,
Like puppies with their puppy; since, a man,
I did as these have done, but did not die—
I will content the people as I can
And give up these to them: Behold the man!

I have suffered, in a dream, because of him,
Many things; for this last saviour, man,
I have lied as I lie now. But what is lying?
Men wash their hands, in blood, as best they can.
I find no fault in this just man.

I don't have any favorite single poem. Perhaps if I were choosing one poem for people to read it would be "The End of the Rainbow," but that is too long for use in your book. "Eighth Air Force" expresses better than any other of the poems I wrote about the war what I felt about the war.

Randall Jarrell

William Stafford

THE FARM ON THE GREAT PLAINS

A telephone line goes cold;
birds tread it wherever it goes.
A farm back of a great plain
tugs an end of the line.

I call that farm every year,
ringing it, listening, still;
no one is home at the farm,
the line gives only a hum.

Some year I will ring the line
on a night at last the right one,
and with an eye tapered for braille
from the phone on the wall

I will see the tenant who waits—
the last one left at the place;
through the dark my braille eye
will lovingly touch his face.

"Hello, is Mother at home?"
No one is home today.
"But Father—he should be there."
No one—no one is here.

"But you—are you the one . . .?"
Then the line will be gone
because both ends will be home:
no space, no birds, no farm.

My self will be the plain,
wise as winter is gray,
pure as cold posts go
pacing toward what I know.

A glance at "The Farm on the Great Plains" jolts me with a succession of regrets about it, but these regrets link with reassurances as I confront and accept something of my portion in writing: an appearance of moral commitment mixed with a deliberate—even a flaunted—nonsophistication; an organized form cavalierly treated; a trace of narrative for company amid too many feelings. There are emergences of consciousness in the poem, and some outlandish lunges for communication; but I can stand quite a bit of this sort of thing if a total poem gives evidence of locating itself.

And the *things* here—plains, farm, home, winter, lavished all over the page—these command my allegiance in a way that is beyond my power to analyze at the moment. Might I hazard that they signal something like austere hope? At any rate, they possess me. I continue to be a willing participant in the feelings and contradictions that led me to write the poem.

William E. Stafford

Henry Rago

THE KNOWLEDGE OF LIGHT

I
The willow shining
From the quick rain,
Leaf, cloud, early star
Are shaken light in this water:
The tremolo of their brightness: light
Sung back in light.

II
The deep shines with the deep.
A deeper sky utters the sky.
These words waver
Between sky and sky.

III
A tree laced of many rivers
Flows into a wide slow darkness
And below the darkness, flowers again
To many rivers that are a tree.

IV
Wrung from silence
Sung in lightning
From stone sprung

The quickening signs
Lines quivered
Numbers flew

Darkness beheld
Darkness and told
Each in each
The depths not darkness.

V
To know
Meaning to celebrate:
Meaning
To become "in some way"
Another; to come
To a becoming:
To have come well.

VI
Earth wakens to the word it wakens.

These dancers turn half-dreaming
Each to the other, glide
Each from a pool of light on either side
Below the dark wings
And flutter slowly, come slowly
Or drift farther again,
Turn to the single note, lifted,
And leap, their whirling lines
Astonished into one lucidity:
Multiples of the arc.

Shapes of the heart!

VII

The year waits at the depth of summer.
The air, the island, and the water
Are drawn to evening. The long month
Is lost in the long evening.

If words could hold this world
They would bend themselves to one
Transparency; if this
Depth of the year, arch of the hour
Came perfect to
The curving of one word
The sound would widen, quietly as from crystal,
Sphere into sphere: candor
Answering a child's candor
Beyond the child's question.

"The Knowledge of Light," first published in 1957, is the central poem in a trilogy which itself seems to me to locate the center of all my poetry thus far. With the other two poems, "A Sky of Late Summer" (1955) and "The Attending" (1957), it contains the best I know.

H. L...y Ra...

John Malcolm Brinnin

HOTEL PARADISO E COMMERCIALE

Another hill town:
another dry Cinzano in the sun.
I couldn't sleep in that enormous echo—
silence and water music, sickly street lamps
neither on nor off—a night
of islands and forgotten languages.

Yet morning, marvelously frank, comes up
with bells, with loaves, with letters
distributed like gifts. I watch a fat priest
spouting grape seeds, a family weeping
in the fumes of a departing bus.

This place is nowhere
except on the map. Wheels spin the sun,
with a white clatter shutters are shut to,
umbrellas bloom in striped and sudden groves.
The day's away, impossibly the same,
and only minutes are at all important—
if women by a wall,
a lean dog and a cheerful humpback
selling gum and ball-points
are important. My glass is empty.
It is Wednesday. It is not going to rain.

Observation
without speculation. How soon
the eye craves what it cannot see,
goes limpid, glazed, unanswerable,
lights on a pigeon walking in a circle,
hangs on a random shadow,
would rather sleep.

How old am I?
What's missing here? What do these people
feed on, that won't feed on them? This town
needs scrolls, celestial delegations,
a swoon of virgins, apostles in apple green,
a landscape riding on a holy shoulder.

The morning stays.
As though I kept an old appointment,
I start by the cats' corridors—*Banco di Roma*,
wineshops, gorgeous butcheries—
toward some mild angel of annunciation,
upstairs, most likely, badly lit,
speaking in rivets on a band of gold.

Praise God, this town keeps one
unheard of masterpiece to justify
a million ordinary mornings,
and pardon this one.

Associations with Italy—the confounding vitality and vast sophis-
tication of its poor; the way in which its backdrops of visible history
make every small human encounter seem dramatic and important—

are a good part of my preference for this poem. Beyond these, I choose it because of a feeling of having made, for myself at least, an observation, perhaps a statement, about the steady, sustaining illumination cast by even minor works of art upon the little sensations and anecdotal substance of every day. Not without surprise, geography confirms the obvious: life is explained and justified in all the ways that bronze and stone, pigment and sound can be made to reflect it; places where these reflections do not exist may be picturesque and diverting but, finally, they are anonymous, "nowhere except on the map."

John Malcolm Brinnin

John Ciardi

SONG FOR AN ALLEGORICAL PLAY

Ah could we wake in mercy's name—
the church mouse in each other's eyes
forgiven, the wart hog washed in flame
confessed—when paunch from paunch we rise,
false and unmartyred, to pretend
we dress for Heaven in the end.

To look and not to look away
from what we see, but, kindly known,
admit our scraping small decay
and the gross jowls of flesh on bone—
think what a sweetness tears might be
in mercy, each by each set free.

Only Success is beast enough
to stop our hearts. Oh twist his tail
and let him howl. When best we love
we have no reason but to fail,
in reason learning as we live
we cannot fail what we forgive.

That mouse is in your eyes and mine.
That wart hog wallows in our blood.
But, ah, let mercy be our sign,

and all our sad beasts, understood,
shall rise, grown admirable, and be,
in mercy, each by each set free.

At first, I was all for this project until I sat down to what I thought would be the happy task of picking out one poem I especially liked and immediately found it to be the most demanding and uncomfortable confusion into which I had ever plunged myself. Surely, I told myself in dismay, I was overdoing something. It wasn't a matter of trying to pick out my "best" poem—I don't see how any one could do that. All that was necessary was to pick out a poem I especially liked for whatever reasons I liked it. But which poem and for what reasons?

Maybe my trouble lay in having written too much. (Can one?) In any case there were too many poems putting forth too many claims upon me. Every poet, I think, dredges himself in hope of bringing to song and form or to saying and form some shape of his own life, a shape brought up from so deep a level in himself that it will suggest to a good reader his own shapes and his own depths. My theory goes one step further: if the shape is truly caught into a poem and if it is from deep enough in me, it cannot help being a shape from everyone else's depths. That, I suppose, is really a Jungian idea.

But a man lives so many lives. I have been driven again and again, for example, to write about my father, actually my unknown father, for he died before I was three, killed in an automobile accident. There is no mystery left in me about the compulsion: my mother in her bereavement changed me into my father until I more than half believed I really was my father transposed. Inevitably, too, the unknown father begins to feel like God. Because all this produced a combination of insanities that were grained into me, I was strongly drawn to choose one of the poems that sprang from that grain, perhaps, "Elegy" ("My father was born with a spade in his hand and traded it"). I could have chosen it and said of it that I believe it finally brought to form in a rhythm that, to my ear at least, truly enforces the saying, an experience fundamental to me.

For related but different reasons, I could have chosen "Three Views of a Mother," and I could have added that the last section of that poem is perhaps the first effort at capturing someone else's voice —dramatically, that is—that strikes me as successful. It was germinal, therefore, for I have found myself more and more drawn to trying to put voices—other voices—into poems.

War was another in-reaching experience and I was drawn to "Elegy Just in Case"—a poem I have revised over and over again for years, and one I am not at all sure I am through revising, but the one, I think, that comes closest to equalling in a self-making form all those mad nights I lay awake and was afraid at the same time that I was half-content because I was able to take my fear out and look at it long enough to put it back with a shrug. Something like that. I may be describing it badly, but the mood of it stays with me.

So for any number of others. It is a mistake of course to like a poem because the experience from which it took off is a dear one. It could be too easy to confuse the personal experience with the experience the poem makes. Yet with many such allowances made and considered I was strongly drawn to both "Men Marry What They Need" and (from "Fragments from Italy") "Nona Domenica Garnaro sits in the sun."

And having thought of so many reasons for which I might have chosen so many other poems, I am not at all sure I know my reasons for the choice I have made.

I like both poems that sing and poems that say. Singing and saying both have their rhythms, and any good rhythm is a joy to find. Basically, I think, I am a "saying" poet. Perhaps I like this Song because it feels successful as a singing poem. How can one fail to be happy about singing?

I feel, too, that it is both in my own voice and in a voice that would do for a play. I think I want to do a poetic play sometime. Perhaps I never shall. Certainly I know too little about theatre to make a playable play, but I have no objection to some sort of closet drama. Except that I incline to shy away from "drama" as the word. I have to be vague here. If I were anything but vague I could get down to work and begin the thing. But I think what I am groping toward is some kind of "enactment," perhaps an "allegorical enactment." A fair question, of course, is—"Enactment of what?" I am tempted to answer "Meaning," but that isn't exact either. Whatever it is will have to form on the dendrites. Let me see if I can do it first. Then, if ever, will be time enough to try to say it.

And finally, despite the dangers of choosing for "subject" reasons, I think this song is my best love poem. It sings me an image, an idea, and a tone I'd like to live by and to keep my loves by. Which is, of course, to claim that poetry is fundamentally a moral thing. I think it is—provided the morality is first alive enough to sing and joyous enough to seek form.

John Ciardi

Peter Viereck

SOME REFRAINS AT THE CHARLES RIVER

I
O sunstruck spray, where change and changeless meet:
    I would abscond to the safe silence
    That hides in the heart of the traffic bustle,
    The easy peace of outwardness.
But sun reached down and knit me back to you.
    River I grew from, river I return to,
    I've dredged you for both sun and moon;
    Knew you, I thought, but now what strangeness?
"I will, thou shalt," says Will; "I will, I will";
I want things blue, and I will have them so—
Till every droplet radiates and savors
Blue, blue, and gold. Most fugitive of golds,
Silvering nightly out of tarnished suns.
Once more: blue, blue, and gold! My words are colors,
On which I float all things that do not flow.

But will rules surfaces and never secrets;
You must escape me till I set you free.

II
O sunstruck spray, where glow and glacial meet:
    I would abscond to the safe silence
    That hides in the heart of the traffic bustle,

The cowardice of action, action.
But sun reached down and knit me back to you.
    River I grew from, river I return to,
    I've traced your white and your yellow script;
    Knew you, but now what overwhelming?
Diphthong of tunes outside the brow and in it,
Single pulse of tides that foam both blue and red,
What truth, what prayer, where wave, where blood are one.
Will wake together—clear, clear, one instant clear—
Our ears and you: great unclear Voice from sky?

But wakefulness commands not shapes but shadows.
I cannot wake you till you teach me sleep.

III
O sunstruck spray,
Here the eternal and the moment meet.
    I would abscond to the safe silence
    That hides in the heart of the traffic bustle,
    The bland dying of liveliness.
But sun reached down and knit me back to you.
    River I grew from, river I belong to,
    Now circling home to gold from silver:—
    What thunder, O familiar stranger?
Jubilant gold of fabulous ablutions,
Gold undulant on quick wet toy-small hills;
Hammerer at lids; pore-drenching wine of light;
From ripply mirrors upward-falling dew,
Here, here, and hovering, round and round my sight;
And of what thunder where "flame" and "shout" are one,
Knitting my nerve-strands to your strands of sun.

But sight sees not the Vision but the view.
I cannot see you till I doubt my eyes.

Too much outwardness dominates our world; poetry and the con-
templation of beauty—for example, a beautiful river—is our refuge
against outwardness. But—even when we achieve the inward, the
spiritual, too much is a forced and willed kind of inwardness; too
much is willed, too much is awake. This prevents true inspiration,
which cannot be kept by imprisoning it or by mere daytime wisdom.
It can be kept only by not trying to keep it, by not subjecting it to
will.

We pass through three stages in advancing toward beauty and
spiritual peace: The lowest stage is the external traffic bustle. This
has mere change and nothing abiding. The second stage is inward and
spiritual, but is willed and daytime; mere top-of-the brain stuff; this
gets mere surfaces. The third stage is the true vision, as opposed to
mere view, mere surface.

The sun-drenched spray of the River Charles is a symbol of true
vision, in both its aspects: the ever changing and the ever changeless.
The sun is unchanging and constant; the river is changing and mov-
ing every second; the sun-drenched spray combines both these as-
pects of our life.

Peter Viereck

Gwendolyn Brooks

From THE CHILDREN OF THE POOR

What shall I give my children? who are poor,
Who are adjudged the leastwise of the land,
Who are my sweetest lepers, who demand
No velvet and no velvety velour;
But who have begged me for a brisk contour,
Crying that they are quasi, contraband
Because unfinished, graven by a hand
Less than angelic, admirable or sure.
My hand is stuffed with mode, design, device.
But I lack access to my proper stone.
And plenitude of plan shall not suffice
Nor grief nor love shall be enough alone
To ratify my little halves who bear
Across an autumn freezing everywhere.

I like this poem for at least two reasons: in it, I feel, is truly the "song" of any children born to find their deprivation beside them; this is coupled, almost made one, with the plaint of parents who "lack access to . . . proper stone."

Gwendolyn Brooks

Charles Causley

A VISIT TO VAN GOGH

at the Asylum of Saint-Paul-du-Mausolée

The French bus halts on the Plateau of Antiques
Unloads its cargo on the sweating square,
The Arch of Glanum, cut with vines and captives,
Explodes in triumph on the Roman air.
In their mausolée, Caius and young Lucius
Watch the white mountain from their cage of bone
And the shot city, untongued by disaster,
Burns on the blue a hundred flames of stone.

Wearing the straw hat of the sun, the mad sun
I strolled the staring sulphur flowers by.
Paint streamed like Christ's blood in the firmament.
Stone-pine and cypress crucified the sky.
An exclamation of black baking olives
Silenced the stunning light. I pulled the bell.
You are, she seemed to say who made an answer,
Seventy years late. Enter. We know you well.

Down in the dead path the whining of a fountain.
Tin voices overhead of birds, bells, clocks.
The awful silence of the pot geranium
At God knows what wrecks on these flowers, these rocks.
In the drowned cloister the white wading rose tree

Wrote on the water's throat its gift of gall,
Lanced with thorn the torn air, the enormous answer
To the cold question of the asylum wall.

A priest with shilling hair, boots and a cycle
Clumped past to benediction, eyes away.
The roof has fallen on the painter's studio.
Is out of bounds. To come another day.
Another day? I crossed, I said, a lifetime
To hold this vine, these olives in my hand.
He hurried with pure pom-faced nuns. *The service*
Must take its usual course, you understand?

You wish to see him? The old woman pointed:
A dusted field-path stitched with oil and vines.
I walked into the golden gape of summer.
The mountain slept, showed prehistoric spines.
Turning, I met the long glare of the madhouse,
A single unbarred stare, a square eye.
See, he is here! It was the old woman, waving
At mountain, meadow, air and tree and sky.

I saw, that storied summer at the bus stop
Under basilicas of birds, a marble eye
Flash from the fettered arch, the trim mausolée
Slung, hard as history, on the heavy sky.
The man ignored, I said, your obvious story.
Did you remark him as he passed you by?
On their proud pillar, Lucius and young Caius
Combed their stone hair, laughed, and made no reply.

I wrote this poem after my first visit to Provence. Reading it recaptures for me more vividly than anything else I wrote at that time my feeling for this sulky and sultry landscape. As usual, I made no notes, kept no diary: for this means always, to me, the death of imaginative realism. I remained unprepared emotionally for what I should find when I arrived at the Plateau des Antiques just outside Saint-Rémy: the ruined Roman city, the triumphal gate, the mausoleum surmounted by the two mysterious stone figures that are possibly memorials to the grandsons of the Emperor Augustus, one of whom died in Spain and the other in Syria. A few hundred yards down the pink, dusty road is the lunatic asylum of Saint-Paul-du-Mausolée, once a monastery, where Vincent van Gogh painted some of his last pictures while a voluntary patient from 1889 to 1890.

I remembered, at this time, no comment in paint by this supreme and distracted genius on the smashed splendours that littered the landscape, though he must have seen them often enough. The ravaged figures, equally, seem to have gazed through him with stone eyes. All that appeared permanent was the blazing landscape of Provence itself. Like van Gogh, I felt a stranger from the north: fascinated as well as frightened by the country's violent rawness. No one, I feel, could visit Provence and remain unhaunted by the fierce ghost of the man to whom Cézanne said, after studying his pictures, "To be honest, they are the paintings of a madman." What is the process that has rendered them finally, as their creator, unbearably sane?

Charles Causley

Joseph Langland

WAR

When my young brother was killed
By a mute and dusty shell in the thorny brush
Crowning the boulders of the Villa Verde Trail
On the island of Luzon,

I laid my whole dry body down,
Dropping my face like a stone in a green park
On the east banks of the Rhine;

On an airstrip skirting the Seine
His sergeant brother sat like a stick in his barracks
While cracks of fading sunlight
Caged the dusty air;

In the rocky rolling hills west of the Mississippi
His father and mother sat in a simple Norwegian parlor
With a photograph smiling between them on the table
And their hands fallen into their laps
Like sticks and dust;

And still other brothers and sisters,
Linking their arms together,
Walked down the dusty road where once he ran
And into the deep green valley

To sit on the stony banks of the stream he loved
And let the murmuring waters
Wash over their blood-hot feet with a springing crown of tears.

I wrote a considerable number of poems on the general subject of war before I did this one. But in this one all the excitement and misery of several years of my life, climaxed by the death of a promising brother, came to rest, ten years after World War II was over. It seemed that its only possible title was "War."

It is not possible for me to say that this poem is typical of how I write or wish to write; it is a residue of a kind of effort, a completion. With this personal and overwhelming subject, my problem was to throw away much that I knew about poetry and yet subtly keep it.

I wanted to come as close as possible to things as they were and yet keep a strict control and proportion of detail and statement, to keep the poem casual and tense, close to prose but purely poetry, flat but singing, dry but emotionally full, to condemn strongly with the quietest reverence. I wanted a series of separate scenes to blend, a group of slow-moving pictures to pace the mind in a serene procession, always singing.

When I received news of my brother's death and began the group of poems which, much later, led to this one, I was fighting with the American infantry in Germany. Art having its generous loyalties, I think it pleases me now that this poem has been set to music by a former infantry officer in the German army and has been published in Hungarian in Budapest since that late revolution was terribly crushed.

So it seems that this poem has made a little entry into the contemporary world; that, too, pleases me. And I learned something basic about my own daily relationship to that world from the long, memorializing, and loving effort of writing this poem.

Joseph Langland

Robert Lowell

FORD MADOX FORD

1873-1939

The lobbed ball plops, then dribbles to the cup . . .
(a birdie Fordie!). But it nearly killed
the ministers. Lloyd George was holding up
the flag. He gabbled, "Hop-toad, hop-toad, hop-toad!
Hueffer has used a niblick on the green;
it's filthy art, Sir, filthy art!"
You answered, "What is art to me and thee?
Will a blacksmith teach a midwife how to bear?"
That cut the puffing statesman down to size,
Ford. You said, "Otherwise,
I would have been general of a division." Ah Ford!
Was it war, the sport of kings, that your *Good Soldier*,
the best French novel in the language, taught
those Georgian Whig magnificoes at Oxford,
at Oxford decimated on the Somme?
Ford, five times black-balled for promotion,
then mustard gassed voiceless some seven miles
behind the lines at Nancy or Belleau Wood:
you emerged in your "worn uniform,
gilt dragons on the revers of the tunic,"
a Jonah—O divorced, divorced
from the whale-fat of post-war London! Boomed,
cut, plucked and booted! In Provence, New York . . .
marrying, blowing . . . nearly dying

at Boulder, when the altitude
pressed the world on your heart,
and your audience, almost football-size,
shrank to a dozen, while you stood
mumbling, with fish-blue-eyes,
and mouth pushed out
fish-fashion, as if you gagged for air. . . .
Sandman! Your face, a childish *O*. The sun
is pernod-yellow and it gilds the heirs
of all the ages there on Washington
and Stuyvesant, your Lilliputian squares,
where writing turned your pockets inside out.
But master, mammoth mumbler, tell me why
the bales of your left-over novels buy
less than a bandage for your gouty foot.
Wheel-horse, O unforgetting elephant,
I hear you huffing at your old Brevoort,
Timon and Falstaff, while you heap the board
for publishers. Fiction! I'm selling short
your lies that made the great your equals. Ford,
you were a kind man and you died in want.

Something planned and grand, and something helter skelter and
unexpected seemed to come together in this poem. I thought for a
long time I would never catch the tone and the man; now I think I
have perhaps.

Bøt Søwll

John Heath-Stubbs

IBYCUS

When the city cast out the best
    In a clamour of indecision,
I had no breath to waste
    Cobbling up their division:
I unhooked the lyre from its peg,
    Turned ship to the Samian shore.
I call no-one to witness
    But the clanging birds of the air.

The quince-tree garden is shattered,
    The vine-shoots fail in spring.
Down from the Thracian mountains
    On fire with the lightning
Love comes, like a blackguard wind.
    Love was betrayal and fear.
I call no man to witness
    But the clanging birds of the air.

The open-handed I praise,
    Great-souled Polycrates,
Pride of whose tinted galleons
    Ruled the Ionian seas.
Treachery took him—nailed
    For the crows to peck him bare.
I call no-one to witness
    But the clanging birds of the air.

Twilight: a narrow place:
    Armed men blocking the path;
Gold glisters on my finger,
    In chevron high overhead
The southward-journeying cranes—
    What Erinnyes are here,
I call no-one to witness
    But the clanging birds of the air.

I feel a certain embarrassment in acceding to the editors' request for a "personal statement" on the poem I have chosen. The reason is this: the very reason why I write poetry at all is that for me a poem is the only really personal statement I can make.

Truthfully, one's favourite among one's own poems is nearly always the poem one has just written. But that mood of enthusiasm may wear off, sometimes very disillusioningly so. I have chosen, therefore, a poem written about a dozen years ago, which for me, if for no one else, has stood the test of time. In fact, I do not think it is one that has particularly recommended itself to my readers. If I remember rightly, it has not been chosen by editors for inclusion in any previous anthology. This may be because, like many of my poems, it is highly allusive and is on a classical subject—and that not one of the very best known ones. I am not quite sure why so many readers today seem to get so annoyed if one writes like that. English poets have always made use of such subjects and allusions. Today we are supposed to be living in a time of universal education. Books on history, archaeology and mythology, as well as the classics themselves in translation sell by their thousands in paper back. This ought to make poems like this one of mine more, and not less, readily accessible than in the past. But it obviously doesn't, and at present I am trying to impose a rationing system on my Muse in regard to such things.

I don't write like this to show how clever and well read I am—though I am rather clever and well read as a matter of fact and I have never thought these were bad things to be. Albeit, I did not have a proper classical education: I have small Latin and less Greek. Nor am I primarily interested in bringing the dead past to life. It is simply that I find myth, history and legend a convenient frame of reference against which to set experiences of contemporary, and yet, I feel, universal, relevance. In this case, the theme of the poet's political dilemma, the poet's freedom, and the poet's fate.

I enjoy contemplating this poem because I feel that I have given these themes a satisfying, concise, and objective form. At the same time, I don't think I have been untrue to the historical poet Ibycus. I have succeeded in incorporating one of the actual fragments of this poet into the second stanza, in very free paraphrase. (The same fragment, by the way, forms the basis of Ezra Pound's poem "Cydonian Spring.")

Finally, I think this poem *sounds*. I find this a good poem for reading aloud and frequently use it as a sort of warming-up piece at the beginning of a reading when I am asked to read my verses in public. The images and of course the incantatory character of the refrain can "get" an audience, so that it doesn't matter if they have only a dim idea who the hell Ibycus was and have no clue to the allusions.

Wm Heath Stubbs

William Jay Smith

GALILEO GALILEI

Comes to knock and knock again
At a small secluded doorway
In the ordinary brain.

Into light the world is turning,
And the clocks are set for six;
And the chimney pots are smoking,
And the golden candlesticks.

Apple trees are bent and breaking,
And the heat is not the sun's;
And the Minotaur is waking,
And the streets are cattle runs.

Galileo Galilei,
In a flowing, scarlet robe,
While the stars go down the river
With the turning, turning globe,

Kneels before a black Madonna
And the angels cluster round
With grave, uplifted faces
Which reflect the shaken ground

And the orchard which is burning,
And the hills which take the light;
And the candles which have melted
On the altars of the night.

Galileo Galilei
Comes to knock and knock again
At a small secluded doorway
In the ordinary brain.

"Galileo Galilei" is one of my own favorites by reason, I think, of the curious circumstances of its composition. In Oxford in 1947 an acquaintance of mine told me one morning that he had awoken the previous night and found that the peculiar happenings of his dream had suggested to him the lines of a poem. He began to write them down, but he could not get beyond the opening:

> Galileo Galilei
> Comes to knock and knock again
> At a small secluded doorway
> In the ordinary brain.

I noted the lines down, and forgot about them until that same night when I found myself unable to sleep. I got up and wrote the poem down more or less as it now appears.

This may all sound suspect—*a la* "Kubla Khan"—but it did really happen. The lines I now realize appealed to me particularly because I had just returned from my first trip to Florence, where I had been staying with friends in Pian dei Giullari, just around the corner from the house in which Galileo was living when Milton came to visit him. I was aware in writing the poem of many impressions of Italy, and of the movement of a kind of *mandala*, the dance of a priest around the altar.

In any case, I was rather pleased with what I had done and showed the result the next morning to my friend. He said indignantly that what I had written had nothing whatever to do with what he had had in mind. *Tant pis*, I replied, then he could certainly not expect to get credit for the lines. He agreed that they were now mine; and we have not met since.

Oddly enough, those readers who have admired the poem have all commented on its strange dreamlike quality.

William Jay Smith

Lawrence Ferlinghetti

NEW YORK—ALBANY

God i had forgotten how
the Hudson burns
in indian autumn
Saugerties
Cocksackie
fall away through
all those trees
The leaves die turning
falling fallen
falling into loam of dark
yellow into death
Disappearing
falling fallen falling
god god those
'pestilence-stricken multitudes'
rushed into the streets
blown all blasted
They are hurting them
with wood rakes
They are raking them
in great hills
They are burning them
lord lord
the leaves curl burning
the curled smoke gives up
to eternity

Never
never the same leaf turn again
the same leaves burn
lord lord
in a red field
a white stallion stands
and pees his oblivion
upon those leaves
washing my bus window
only now blacked out
by a covered bridge
we flash through
only once
No roundtrip ticket
Lord lord never returning
the youth years fallen
away back then
Under the Linden trees in Boston Common
Lord Lord
Trees think
through these woods of years
They flame forever
with those thoughts
Lord Lord
i did not see eternity
the other night
but now in burning
turning day
Lord Lord Lord
every bush burns
Love licks
all down

All gone
in the red end
Lord Lord Lord Lord
Small nuts fall
Mine too

"New York-Albany" is a favorite poem of mine because it fills a central moment in the middle of the journey of my life when I came to myself in a dark wood. . . .

lawrence ferlinghetti

William Meredith

ON FALLING ASLEEP TO BIRDSONG

In a tree at the edge of the clearing
A whippoorwill calls in the dark,
An American forest bird.
Lying in bed I hear him;
He is old, or at least no answer
Comes from the wood behind him;
I lose him there in the topmost
Invisible twigs in my head.

At the edge of the town I grow old
On a farm, sooner or later.
Lying alone at night
I remember my father and mother;
I see them, not tossing together
In their concern over me
But propped on separate pillows,
Going away like trees
A leaf at a time and angry
At the wingless, terrible trip;
And asking if they can stay.

I thrash in bed at forty
Reluctant to go on that trip.
I conjure nightingales
With their lovely lecherous song;

This is a question of will
And I conjure those silky birds
Tossing the boughs like bedsprings,
Fluting themselves to death
In music that will not cool.
Ah. I liked it better
With the randy foreign fowl
When summer had her fill.
But I am in bed in the fall
And cannot arrest the dream
That unwinds a chase and a rape
And ends in Thracian pain.

Although no bird comes,
The whippoorwill does not mourn.
At the bourn of human farms
He holds a constant song;
When time has gone away
He calls to what he calls.
Dark bird, we will prevail
If life indeed is one—
The fluting time and now,
Now and the pillow-time
Propped with knowledge and pain.
If some dark call repeats
And means the same and more,
The rest I will endure.
If it is one, dark bird
Who watch my middle sleep,
I will grow old, as a man
Will read of a transformation:
Knowing it is a fable
Contrived to answer a question

Answered, if ever, in fables,
Yet all of a piece and clever
And at some level, true.

A poet with any modesty at all has to shake off both his modesty and the sense of partial failure that hangs over even his favorite poem before he says, I like this one. Shaking these off, I can speak warmly about "Falling Asleep to Birdsong" for two reasons. First, I think it *sounds like* what it is saying. To my ear, anyhow, the music of the lines goes along with the melancholy and finally the affirmation of the story. The story is about a man, myself, who thinks about his middle age, his parents, death, sexual love and old age, all in the context of the title. And in some lucky way, and to my ear if to nobody else's, the sound of the verse accompanies and strengthens the changes of feeling—which is, of course, the least you can ask of prosody.

I expect it would be possible to write something here about the effect of trimeter lines, feminine endings and occasional anapestic feet. But analysis of poetry in those terms has never seemed to me to prove anything very serious, either about the success of a poem, or about the emotion it contains, or about how it was made. I wouldn't scan a poem while I was doing its important work—the first couple of drafts—any more than I would refer to a marriage manual at a critical moment: if the instinct fails, so will the act.

The second reason I like the poem is that it was what Robert Frost has somewhere called a *gatherer*. It pulled together a lot of apparently unrelated experience as it declared itself. My father had recently died. I had bought an old farm. I hadn't written a poem for some time. I was about to be forty. I had been reading and thinking about the fable of Philomela which haunts English poetry as an image of love and lust. My mind was not free, as whose ever is, of erotic recollection and fantasy. And I had been thinking about how unready I was either to grow old or to die. Then this poem was touched off by the nightsong of a clean-living, self-sufficient American bird, a whip-poorwill. In my rather categorical mind these disparate ideas fused, at the edge of sleep, into the vision of acceptance the poem ends with.

William Meredith

Reed Whittemore

REFLECTIONS UPON A RECURRENT SUGGESTION BY CIVIL DEFENSE AUTHORITIES THAT I BUILD A BOMBSHELTER IN MY BACKYARD

I remember a dug-out we dug in the backyard as children
And closed on top with an old door covered with dirt
And sat in hour by hour, thoroughly squashed
But safe, with our chins on our knees, from the world's hurt.
There, as the earth trickled down on us as in an hour glass,
Our mothers called us, called us to come and be fed,
But we would not, could not hear them, possessed as we were
By our self's damp stronghold among the selfless dead.

This and a few other fantasies of my youth
I remember now as scenes in a marathon play
That plunged on for act after act with the lost hero
Preferring, to death, some brave kind of decay.
While he was still on stage I grew up
And sneaked away as he battered his hemlock cup.

Now, they say, willy nilly I must go back,
And under the new and terrible rules of romance
Dig yet another hole in which like a child
My adult soul may trifle with circumstance.
But I'll not, no, not do it, not go back

And lie there in that dark under the weight
Of all that earth on that old door for my state.
I know too much to think now that, if I creep
From the grown-up's house to the child's house, I'll keep.

I like this one partly out of malice toward the editors of *The New Yorker*, who rejected it six or seven years ago on the grounds that while they liked it it was no longer timely. There may have been other reasons—rejection slips are seldom honest—but I prefer not to think of them. Though the second stanza is weak (I wouldn't change it now) the rest of it still seems o.k. to me, and three lines in the last stanza are among the best I've written (that makes them really hot, of course):

> But I'll not, no, not do it, not go back
> And lie there in that dark under the weight
> Of all that earth on that old door for my state.

I'll probably never follow those instructions in an emergency, but I like to think I would; so the poem gives me a pleasant image of me as I would like to be—what more could a poet want from his own lines?

Reed Whittemore

Howard Nemerov

RUNES

. . . *insaniebam salubriter et moriebar vitaliter.*
St. Augustine

I

This is about the stillness in moving things,
In running water, also in the sleep
Of winter seeds, where time to come has tensed
Itself, enciphering a script so fine
Only the hourglass can magnify it, only
The years unfold its sentence from the root.
I have considered such things often, but
I cannot say I have thought deeply of them:
That is my theme, of thought and the defeat
Of thought before its object, where it turns
As from a mirror, and returns to be
The thought of something and the thought of thought,
A trader doubly burdened, commercing
Out of one stillness and into another.

II

About Ulysses, the learned have reached two
Distinct conclusions. In one, he secretly
Returns to Ithaca, is recognized
By Euryclea, destroys the insolent suitors,
And makes himself known to Penelope,
Describing the bed he built; then, at the last

Dissolve, we see him with Telemachus
Leaving the palace, planning to steal sheep:
The country squire resumes a normal life.
But in the other, out beyond the gates
Of Hercules, gabbling persuasively
About virtue and knowledge, he sails south
To disappear from sight behind the sun;
Drowning near blessed shores he flames in hell.
I do not know which ending is the right one.

III
Sunflowers, traders rounding the horn of time
Into deep afternoons, sleepy with gain,
The fall of silence has begun to storm
Around you where you nod your heavy heads
Whose bare poles, raking out of true, will crack,
Driving your wreckage on the world's lee shore.
Your faces no more will follow the sun,
But bow down to the ground with a heavy truth
That dereliction learns, how charity
Is strangled out of selfishness at last;
When, golden misers in the courts of summer,
You are stripped of gain for coining images
And broken on this quarter of the wheel,
It is on savage ground you spill yourselves,
And spend the tarnished silver of your change.

IV
The seed sleeps in the furnaces of death,
A cock's egg slept till hatching by a serpent
Wound in his wintry coil, a spring so tight
In his radical presence that every tense
Is now. Out of this head the terms of kind,

Distributed in syntax, come to judgment,
Are basilisks who write our sentences
Deep at the scripture's pith, in rooted tongues,
How one shall marry while another dies.
Give us our ignorance, the family tree
Grows upside down and shakes its heavy fruit,
Whose buried stones philosophers have sought.
For each stone bears the living word, each word
Will be made flesh, and all flesh fall to seed:
Such stones from the tree; and from the stones, such blood.

V

The fat time of the year is also time
Of the Atonement; birds to the berry bushes,
Men to the harvest; a time to answer for
Both present plenty and emptiness to come.
When the slain legal deer is salted down,
When apples smell like goodness, cold in the cellar,
You hear the ram's horn sounded in the high
Mount of the Lord, and you lift up your eyes
As though by this observance you might hide
The dry husk of an eaten heart which brings
Nothing to offer up, no sacrifice
Acceptable but the canceled-out desires
And satisfactions of another year's
Abscess, whose zero in His winter's mercy
Still hides the undecipherable seed.

VI

White water now in the snowflake's prison,
A mad king in a skullcap thinks these thoughts
In regular hexagons, each one unlike
Each of the others. The atoms of memory,

Like those that Democritus knew, have hooks
At either end, but these? Insane tycoon,
These are the riches of order snowed without end
In this distracted globe, where is no state
To fingerprint the flakes or number these
Moments melting in flight, seeds mirroring
Substance without position or a speed
And course unsubstanced. What may the spring be,
Deep in the atom, among galactic snows,
But the substance of things hoped for, argument
Of things unseen? White water, fall and fall.

VII

Unstable as water, thou shalt not excel
—Said to the firstborn, the dignity and strength,
And the defiler of his father's bed.
Fit motto for a dehydrated age
Nervously watering whisky and stock,
Quick-freezing dreams into realities.
Brain-surgeons have produced the proustian syndrome,
But patients dunk their tasteless madeleines
In vain, those papers that the Japanese
Amused themselves by watering until
They flowered and became Combray, flower
No more. The plastic and cosmetic arts
Unbreakably record the last word and
The least word, till sometimes even the Muse,
In her transparent raincoat, resembles a condom.

VIII

To go low, to be as nothing, to die,
To sleep in the dark water threading through
The fields of ice, the soapy, frothing water

That slithers under the culvert below the road,
Water of dirt, water of death, dark water,
And through the tangle of the sleeping roots
Under the coppery cold beech woods, the green
Pinewoods, and past the buried hulls of things
To come, and humbly through the breathing dreams
Of all small creatures sleeping in the earth;
To fall with the weight of things down on the one
Still ebbing stream, to go on to the end
With the convict hunted through the swamp all night.
The dog's corpse in the ditch, to come at last
Into the pit where zero's eye is closed.

IX

In this dehydrated time of digests, pills
And condensations, the most expensive presents
Are thought to come in the smallest packages:
In atoms, for example. There are still
To be found, at carnivals, men who engrave
The Lord's Prayer on a grain of wheat for pennies,
But they are a dying race, unlike the men
Now fortunate, who bottle holy water
In plastic tears, and bury mustard seeds
In lucite lockets, and for safety sell
To be planted on the dashboard of your car
The statues, in durable celluloid,
Of Mary and St. Christopher, who both
With humble power in the world's floodwaters
Carried their heavy Savior and their Lord.

X

White water, white water, feather of a form
Between the stones, is the race run to stay

Or pass away? Your utterance is riddled,
Rainbowed and clear and cold, tasting of stone,
Its brilliance blinds me. But still I have seen,
White water, at the breaking of the ice,
When the high places render up the new
Children of water and their tumbling light
Laughter runs down the hills, and the small fist
Of the seed unclenches in the day's dazzle,
How happiness is helpless before your fall,
White water, and history is no more than
The shadows thrown by clouds on mountainsides,
A distant chill, when all is brought to pass
By rain and birth and rising of the dead.

XI

A holy man said to me, "Split the stick
And there is Jesus." When I split the stick
To the dark marrow and the splintery grain
I saw nothing that was not wood, nothing
That was not God, and I began to dream
How from the tree that stood between the rivers
Came Aaron's rod that crawled in front of Pharaoh,
And came the rod of Jesse flowering
In all the generations of the Kings,
And came the timbers of the second tree,
The sticks and yardarms of the holy three-
masted vessel whereon the Son of Man
Hung between thieves, and came the crown of thorns,
The lance and ladder, when was shed that blood
Streamed in the grain of Adam's tainted seed.

XII
Consider how the seed lost by a bird

Will harbor in its branches most remote
Descendants of the bird; while everywhere
And unobserved, the soft green stalks and tubes
Of water are hardening into wood, whose hide,
Gnarled, knotted, flowing, and its hidden grain,
Remember how the water is streaming still.
Now does the seed asleep, as in a dream
Where time is compacted under pressures of
Another order, crack open like stone
From whose division pours a stream, between
The raindrop and the sea, running in one
Direction, down, and gathering in its course
That bitter salt which spices us the food
We sweat for, and the blood and tears we shed.

XIII
There sailed out on the river, Conrad saw,
The dreams of men, the seeds of commonwealths,
The germs of Empire. To the ends of the earth
One many-veined bloodstream swayed the hulls
Of darkness gone, or darkness still to come,
And sent its tendrils steeping through the roots
Of wasted continents. That echoing pulse
Carried the ground swell of all sea-returns
Muttering under history, and its taste,
Saline and cold, was as a mirror of
The taste of human blood. The sailor leaned
To lick the mirror clean, the somber and
Immense mirror that Conrad saw, and saw
The other self, the sacred Cain of blood
Who would seed a commonwealth in the Land of Nod.

XIV

There is a threshold, that meniscus where
The strider walks on drowning waters, or
That tense, curved membrane of the camera's lens
Which darkness holds against the battering light
And the distracted drumming of the world's
Importunate plenty.—Now that threshold,
The water of the eye where the world walks
Delicately, is as a needle threaded
From the reel of a raveling stream, to stitch
Dissolving figures in a watered cloth,
A damask either-sided as the shroud
Of the lord of Ithaca, labored at in light,
Destroyed in darkness, while the spidery oars
Carry his keel across deep mysteries
To harbor in unfathomable mercies.

XV

To watch water, to watch running water
Is to know a secret, seeing the twisted rope
Of runnels on the hillside, the small freshets
Leaping and limping down the tilted field
In April's light, the green, grave and opaque
Swirl in the millpond where the current slides
To be combed and carded silver at the fall;
It is a secret. Or it is not to know
The secret, but to have it in your keeping,
A locked box, Bluebeard's room, the deathless thing
Which it is death to open. Knowing the secret,
Keeping the secret—herringbones of light

Ebbing on beaches, the huge artillery
Of tides—it is not knowing, it is not keeping,
But being the secret hidden from yourself.

Asked to choose a favorite from among my own poems I chose "Runes." My reasons for doing so have of course nothing to do with the reader's judgment as to the success or failure of the poem, but they are somewhat as follows.

It is a poem which attempts much, wants much of its reader as it wanted much of its author. In two ways it represents for me a summary and a climax of many years, a summary concentrated enough, I hope, in spite of its length. First, it was written in a fortnight of continuous devotion, which remains in my memory as a time of great delight; the true happiness in "being a poet" comes when one is able to write thus from the midst of some sustaining center, whose variations and examinations become the poem. Arranging the pieces in what I considered to be their proper order, and eliminating almost as many again as the fifteen which made the final version, occupied a good deal more time than the writing. Second, the substance of the piece is for me a summary of many years' partial preoccupation with its subjects and illustrations: the end of something; hopefully, at the same time, the beginning of something else. It is a bookish poem, as I am a bookish person, with its passing thoughts of St. Paul, Homer, Dante, and many others: those who like the poem will perhaps also like this about it, while those who dislike it will very likely find one of their reasons there; that doesn't matter. But it matters to me, that this expression of mine should have included an element of acknowledgment to certain masters: probably I am fortunate that they are unable to reply.

Finally, this. My friends, to mention no others, have so frequently referred to my poems as "meditative" rather than "dramatic," clearly implying (when not indeed saying) that mine was an inferior form of art, that it gives me a certain backhanded pleasure to allow the justice of their contention in this poem, of which the announced intent is to meditate. Its form is perhaps allied with music: a theme and variations, as in the earlier sequence, "The Scales of the Eyes." And yet it is a drama, with its orderly progression from statement through dispute to resolution. Here, though, lest I begin interpreting the poem, I had best stop.

Howard Nemerov

James Schevill

A STORY OF SOUTINE

Soutine the Sour,
Kindled by Rembrandt's "Woman Bathing,"
Searched for a country model, and at last
Found a peasant woman working in a field,
Her shovel feet bare in the dust.

When he prodded her
To pose, she thought him a snatchy lecher
Until she sensed the mystery of a man
Who had painted only one nervous nude;
Then she thought him mad.

But persuaded by pay,
Glumped bare-footed into the brook,
Skirt held up by her brick-red hands,
Staring at old chucklehead, the painter,
The fury of his cozening face.

For days he slaved,
Commanding the cloddish, fleshly shape
To flow fiercely in colors on the canvas.
Then, one afternoon, crooked cumulus clouds
Gathered for a grimace of rain.

The peasant woman cried
For permission to run from her ponderous pose,
But he shouted at the cramps of her shivering body,
"Stand still!"—or she would be shocked by God
    For the ruined work.

Through the riddling rain,
Thunder clapped and rammed into the driving darkness,
But Soutine painted on with the acid of vision.
At last the paint subsided, and his wilful eyes
    Woke in the dark of his dream-land.

Blue and blubbering in the
Brook, the sodden peasant woman howled hysterically,
And from the rain-wet, singing surge of its colors,
The painting stared at her mortal behavior, reflecting
    The arrogant mirror of art.

Favorite poems often vanish from memory, as they imply a singular love, and a poet's love must be plural for all of his experiments; otherwise, he is dead. So I have merely selected one of my poems which resulted from a question that has haunted me for a long time: Why should poetry relinquish to prose the most interesting subject matter? Contemporary poetry has focused mainly on short, lyrical forms and given up much of its narrative and dramatic force to fiction and biography. In attempting to restore some of this narrative and dramatic force in my own work, I have tried to write many poems based on dramatic events in the lives of famous and infamous people. I wanted to revive some of the relationship between poetry and biography, to create characters with weight and depth. My concern with playwriting was a factor here too. Several of these poems

I thought of as "poem-biographies," as they attempted through the compressive power of poetry to shape and define the major events of my character's life.

My poem, "A Story of Soutine," arose from these experiments with "poem-biographies." It is based on a true incident in Soutine's life, his encounter with a suspicious peasant woman whom he persuaded to pose for him. In the end, it was the conflict between life and art that absorbed me; how often art takes a cruel advantage of innocence and drives mercilessly towards its end. Building the form out of the strange sequence of events, I finally hit upon an experimental, five-line stanza, which could focus the events dramatically, and yet contain enough rhythmic variety so that the images would not be clamped into a too lyrical, regular pattern. This poem needed a blunt, eccentric flow to fit the grotesque struggle between Soutine and the peasant woman. Somehow, I derived great excitement from this experiment, and other similar ones, and I hope some of the excitement is communicated in the poem.

J. Scherill

Richard Wilbur

A BAROQUE WALL-FOUNTAIN
IN THE VILLA SCIARRA
For Dore and Adja

    Under the bronze crown
Too big for the head of the stone cherub whose feet
    A serpent has begun to eat,
Sweet water brims a cockle and braids down

    Past spattered mosses, breaks
On the tipped edge of a second shell, and fills
    The massive third below. It spills
In threads then from the scalloped rim, and makes

    A scrim or summery tent
For a faun-ménage and their familiar goose.
    Happy in all that ragged, loose
Collapse of water, its effortless descent

    And flatteries of spray,
The stocky god upholds the shell with ease,
    Watching, about his shaggy knees,
The goatish innocence of his babes at play;

His fauness all the while
Leans forward, slightly, into a clambering mesh
    Of water-lights, her sparking flesh
In a saecular ecstasy, her blinded smile

    Bent on the sand floor
Of the trefoil pool, where ripple-shadows come
    And go in swift reticulum,
More addling to the eye than wine, and more

    Interminable to thought
Than pleasure's calculus. Yet since this all
    Is pleasure, flash, and waterfall,
Must it not be too simple? Are we not

    More intricately expressed
In the plain fountains that Maderna set
    Before St. Peter's—the main jet
Struggling aloft until it seems at rest

    In the act of rising, until
The very wish of water is reversed,
    That heaviness borne up to burst
In a clear, high, cavorting head, to fill

    With blaze, and then in gauze
Delays, in a gnatlike shimmering, in a fine
    Illumined version of itself, decline,
And patter on the stones its own applause?

     If that is what men are
Or should be, if those water-saints display
     The pattern of our areté,*
What of these showered fauns in their bizarre,

     Spangled, and plunging house?
They are at rest in fulness of desire
     For what is given, they do not tire
Of the smart of the sun, the pleasant water-douse

     And riddled pool below,
Reproving our disgust and our ennui
     With humble insatiety.
Francis, perhaps, who lay in sister snow

     Before the wealthy gate
Freezing and praising, might have seen in this
     No trifle, but a shade of bliss—
That land of tolerable flowers, that state

     As near and far as grass
Where eyes become the sunlight, and the hand
     Is worthy of water: the dreamt land
Toward which all hungers leap, all pleasures pass.

If you have a certain number of Anglo-Saxon generations behind
you, you will feel obliged to work an eight-hour day even in Rome.
When I lived in that city, I used to walk each morning from my
apartment on the Gianicolo to a studio in the garden of the American

* Note: areté, a Greek word meaning, roughly, "virtue."

Academy, passing very often a charming sixteenth- or seventeenth-century fountain. This fountain appeared to me the very symbol or concretion of Pleasure; I felt reproached by it for my Puritanical industry; and at last I compromised with it by making it the subject of a poem.

I like it when the ideas of a poem seem to be necessary aspects of the things or actions which it presents—stretching away and yet always adhering, like shadows. In this case, I may have come near that desideratum.

Richard Wilbur

Kingsley Amis

AFTER GOLIATH

What shall be done to the man
that killeth this Philistine?
I Sam. xvii, 27

The first shot out of that sling
Was enough to finish the thing:
The champion laid out cold
Before half the programmes were sold.
And then, what howls of dismay
From his fans in their dense array:
From aldermen, adjutants, aunts,
Administrators of grants,
Assurance-men, auctioneers,
Advisers about careers,
And advertisers, of course,
Plus the obvious b——s in force—
The whole reprehensible throng
Ten times an alphabet strong.
But such an auspicious debut
Was a little too good to be true,
Our victor sensed; the applause
From those who supported his cause
Sounded shrill and excessive now,
And who were they, anyhow?

Academics, actors who lecture,
Apostles of architecture,
Ancient-gods-of-the-abdomen men,
Angst-pushers, adherents of Zen,
Alastors, austenites, A-test
Abolishers—even the straightest
Of issues looks pretty oblique
When a movement turns into a clique,
The conqueror mused, as he stopped
By the sword his opponent had dropped:
Trophy, or means of attack
On the rapturous crowd at his back?
He shrugged and left it, resigned
To a new battle, fought in the mind,
For faith that his quarrel was just,
That the right man lay in the dust.

I wrote this poem three years ago and I can still read it without irritation (except perhaps at lines 4, 13 and 34). In fact, it gives me pleasure, not as much as when I first read it through after completing it, but still some. It hits off to my own satisfaction something I had been trying to get said for a long time: that there is a disappointing lack of contrast between the enemies of progress (in any field: social, literary, political) and those theoretically on the side of progress. I am glad I managed to get in without too much fuss the qualifying idea that this applies to everyone, including the David-figure, who ends up half-sympathizing with Goliath and obviously is pretty certain to be the next generation's Goliath.

The theme had been on my mind, but a more important reason

why I chose this poem is that it had been kicking around in draft form for months before I felt I had it right. I rewrote it so many times I despaired of it. For a long time the form was wrong; it used to begin

> *Earlier champions of such a cause*
> *Had soldiered through dismemberment, and won.*

To have worked on a poem a lot says nothing about its final merit, but poets are likely not to feel that. "It may not be much good but at least it wasn't easy" is a natural reaction against romantic inspirational attitudes. Regarding poetry as hard work, though perhaps dangerous, strikes me as less dangerous than feeling it ought to possess or obsess one, etc. But don't take my word for it.

Kingsley Amis

Donald Davie

CORRIB. AN EMBLEM

Hairless and worse than leathery, the skin
Of the great ogre, Connemara, mounded
Silvery, fathoms thick. Within
The crook of tutelary arm that cradled
The Corrib's urn, the subcutaneous waters
In their still blue as bright as blood shone out,
By healed-up puckers where his pre-divinity
Was scored and trenched. To him suppose a Daphne
Pursued by art Palladian, picturesque,
Or else Hispanic through the Galway Lynches,
Merchant adventurers turning Medici,
Virtú in freight. Underneath his shoulder
Syrinx, the villa seen across the lough,
A reed now broken, flourished. In his hand
A nymph took root, and here and there a laurel.

Only one other person, so far as I know, ever liked this poem as much as I like it myself. Most people it seems are baffled by it, find it obscure; and in deference to their wishes I left it out when I selected from previous volumes for a *New & Selected Poems*. Yet it is a poem I am proud of, and one that I should like to have remembered. I should not be proud of it if I did not feel that the obscurity others find in it is not my fault, nor theirs, but the fault of history. For the poem depends on an artistic convention familiar to educated men of the seventeenth and eighteenth centuries which has not apparently survived into the educated minds of the present century, though when I wrote the poem I thought it had. This is the convention of representing a river, in sculpture and painting more than in literature, by an image of the river-god reclining across an urn from which flow the waters of his stream; my immediate source was a painting by Tiepolo, but now even more than when I wrote the poem I feel that the whole effect would be ruined if I introduced a reference to Tiepolo by name. For what I want is the impersonality which only such well-established conventions can give, and to allude to Tiepolo would make the poem personal in a very damaging way indeed, as the utterance of a person elaborately well-informed, an intellectual snob, culture-vulture and aesthete. Even more important than the impersonality such a convention can give, is the conciseness; for I could not by any other means have packed into my poem so much information about the history as well as the landscape of the part of Ireland I was writing about. As for the feelings in the poem I suppose they are, first, a feeling for the edge of Europe—for the way in which the nobility and the pathos of European civilisation is nowhere so evident as where it survives at the extreme frontier; and in the second place an apprehension of the tragedy of historical change. The convention, I believe, permits me to make these points without an irrelevant and self-regarding nostalgia.

Donald Davie

Anthony Hecht

THE VOW

In the third month, a sudden flow of blood.
The mirth of tabrets ceaseth, and the joy
Also of the harp. The frail image of God
Lay spilled and formless. Neither girl nor boy,
But yet blood of my blood, nearly my child.
      All that long day
Her pale face turned to the window's mild
        Featureless grey.

And for some nights she whimpered as she dreamed
The dead thing spoke, saying: "Do not recall
Pleasure at my conception. I am redeemed
From pain and sorrow. Mourn rather for all
Who breathlessly issue from the bone gates,
      The gates of horn,
For truly it is best of all the fates
      Not to be born.

"Mother, a child lay gasping for bare breath
On Christmas Eve, when Santa Claus had set
Death in the stocking, and the lights of death
Flamed in the tree. O, if you can, forget
You were the child, turn to my father's lips
      Against the time
When his cold hand puts forth its fingertips
      Of jointed lime."

Doctors of Science, what is man that he
Should hope to come to a good end? *The best
Is not to have been born.* And could it be
That Jewish diligence and Irish jest
The consent of flesh and a midwinter storm
          Had reconciled,
Was yet too bold a mixture to inform
          A simple child?

Even as gold is tried, Gentile and Jew.
If that ghost was a girl's, I swear to it:
Your mother shall be far more blessed than you.
And if a boy's, I swear: The flames are lit
That shall refine us; they shall not destroy
          A living hair.
Your younger brothers shall confirm in joy
          This that I swear.

It's curiously embarrassing for a poet to sit down and say why he likes his own poem, especially if he feels the chances are that on the whole he probably likes it better than almost anybody else. I suppose I would nominate "The Vow" for this anthology, and for a number of odd reasons. For one thing, I like the idea of having a child so young as to be yet unborn speak with all the aged, bitter, Sophoclean wisdom of the great chorus in "Oedipus at Colonus." This is not just being tricky and paradoxical; you are meant to feel that the child, being somehow prior to life (in some Wordsworthian realm of glory, perhaps) and also dead, has a source of special knowledge that entitles it to make such formidable pronouncements. It is in a double sense separated from the world of the living. So there is something very cold-blooded about the way it talks.

When I first thought of writing "The Vow" I remembered a poem on this subject by Robert Lowell which appeared in his first book, *Land of Unlikeness*. I decided not to look at his (and I only dimly remembered it) until I had finished my own, lest I be even unconsciously influenced by mood or tone. I did look at his after mine was done, and was glad to see how different they were, but I feel I still owe him a debt of gratitude for giving me by his example the courage to tackle a difficult and unpleasant subject.

Also, I think the poem needs to be defended against being either praised or blamed for the wrong reasons—these being chiefly that it is "personal," i.e., "bravely confessional," i.e., "true" in some important documentary way that other poems don't try to be, and that this is part of its power or weakness, depending on which view you take. Just how much of it is true in that particular sense I take to be my own private business, though I think it might be objected that the poem ends on a vow so audacious as to smack rather of hubris.

Anthony Hecht

Philip Larkin

ABSENCES

Rain patters on a sea that tilts and sighs.
Fast-running floors, collapsing into hollows,
Tower suddenly, spray-haired. Contrariwise,
A wave drops like a wall: another follows,
Wilting and scrambling, tirelessly at play
Where there are no ships and no shallows.

Above the sea, the yet more shoreless day,
Riddled by wind, trails lit-up galleries:
They shift to giant ribbing, sift away.

Such attics cleared of me! Such absences!

I suppose I like "Absences" (a) because of its subject matter—I am always thrilled by the thought of what places look like when I am not there; (b) because I fancy it sounds like a different, better poet rather than myself. The last line, for instance, sounds like a slightly unconvincing translation from a French symbolist. I wish I could write like this more often.

Incidentally, an oceanographer wrote to me pointing out that I was confusing two kinds of wave, plunging waves and spilling waves, which seriously damaged the poem from a technical viewpoint. I am sorry about this, but do not see how to amend it now.

Philip Larkin

Howard Moss

GOING TO SLEEP IN THE COUNTRY

The terraces rise and fall
As the light strides up and rides over
The hill I see from my window.
The spring in the dogwood now,
Enlarging its small preconceptions,
Puts itself away for the night.
The mountains do nothing but sit,
Waiting for something to happen—
Perhaps for the sky to open.

In the distance, a waterfall,
More sound than vision from here,
Is weighing itself again,
A sound you can hardly hear.
The birds of the day disappear,
As if the darkness were final.
The harder it is to see,
The louder the waterfall.

And then the whippoorwill
Begins its tireless, cool,
Calm, and precise lament—
Again and again and again—
Its love replying in kind,
Or blindly sung to itself,
Waiting for something to happen.

In that rain-prickle of song,
The waterfall stays its sound,
Diminishing like a gong
Struck by the weakening hand
Of a walker walking away,
Who is farther away each time,

Until it is finally dumb.
Each star, at a different depth,
Shines down. The moon shines down.
The night comes into its own,
Waiting for nothing to happen.

"Going to Sleep in the Country" arrived without struggle, apparently without forethought, as if it had been waiting in the wings. I had been working on a longer poem, using cadences rather than strict meter. In the middle of writing this longer poem, the first stanza of "Going to Sleep," minus one line, suddenly appeared. The fifth line of this stanza was the difficult one. I wanted an abstract word like "preconceptions" at this point, but it was a long time in coming.

With the exception of the fifth line of stanza 1, the other stanzas came more or less by themselves through the end of stanza 4. I was surprised, on reading the poem over, to notice that each stanza was one line shorter than the one before. I had not consciously planned it that way but it added to the effect of going to sleep, the waking world growing not only more distant as the poem went on but the sleeper's relationship to it becoming briefer each time. I set out deliberately to make the last stanza five lines long in keeping with the pattern that had naturally developed.

"Going to Sleep in the Country" was for me a kind of reward, as if the struggle and labor of other poems had paid off in this almost effortless one, as if a great deal of conscious training had finally been put to use without my having to do much more than transcribe what the past had stored up.

Considering how the poem came into being, it was of special interest to me that, like a dream, it merged three landscapes—all in New York State—into one. The terraces and mountains come from Millbrook; the waterfall is at Stonypoint; and the whippoorwill sang at Fire Island Pines.

Howard Moss

Daniel G. Hoffman

1956

That week the fall was opulent. Vendanges,
    Dancing, sunlight, autumn warmth, full larder
    Before the endurable oncome of the winter.

Needing a haircut, I asked the coiffeur again
    To cut it short. He shrugged, but, being genial,
    Complied. A Sampson came in for his marcel.

Musique au radio cut short: Shrill voice:
    Our fleet en route to liberate Suez!
    Nasser, beware! Victory in two days!

Then glory used up all the largest type fonts
    As Napoleonic ghosts in parachutes
    Converged canalward on those camel-troops.

Coiffeur and Sampson were ready for the glory.
    But Egyptians, seeing Israel's guns, skedaddled
    Before the Indo-China vets embattled

Them. The RAF pounded the desert
    For two days. Meanwhile John Foster Dulles
    (My countryman) put through long distance calls

To God again, and passed The Moral Law
    Again. Texas and Oklahoma cheered
    His oil on troubled water. It appeared.

OK to Moscow too; peace took the UN
    By unsurprise. Beaten yet once again,
    Dienbienphu yet unavenged, Pétain

Yet unavenged, Verdun . . . My hair grew longer.
    I went to the coiffeur again. This day
    In short supply I found l'amitié.

I spoke of soccer, not Suez, nor glory.
    His shears yet jabbed my head most dangerously.
    The next man up read *Le Combat* sullenly.

L'amitié is scarce. A run on soap.
    Hoarders have got the rice. There's no coal
    In the coalyards. At the school, no oil;

What's plenty? A pyramid in the Magasin
    Of canned-for-America grapefruit, tin on tin;
    A sign says: 'PAMPLEMOUSSES ISRAËLEENES.'

The ration of gas threatens the Cabinet.
    Canal-boats on the Ouche fray weedy hausers.
    Nobody mentions glory now, or the Gaza,

But curses the malign sphynx of history.
    By the Arc de Triomphe they await who'll unriddle the
        past
    And may, even now, be descending the mountain path.

A representative poem . . . that's hard. But a favorite's another matter. I like this one partly because of the pleasure I had in writing it. Every poem proves a pleasure of course, no matter the pains it cost, if in the end it does its work. That is to say ineluctably what one must and cannot in any other way justly express. I hope "1956" does this. It pleases me, too, because it clarified confused emotions felt in a time of intensity and apparent danger. The poem is based on some trivial and tremendous things that happened during the fall when I was the American professor at Dijon. I enjoy the disparity in the scale of its statements. But for five years after, these events didn't show me the pattern that both got right the feeling of the things happening and revealed their relation to one another. Not until we were about to return to Europe; and then a dozen poems came out in a three-month spurt. Then that whole year in Burgundy passed through my mind with such immediacy that I could actually smell the hoarfrost hanging on the fruit trees, and hear the rooster yodeling over the steaming dungpiles in the farmyards in our village. Then my resurrected memories gave me those that belonged in poems and defined what our life was that year. It was an island of time made vivid by distance and the refining away of inessentials. That's what had to be waited for, since while they are happening all things make insistent claims of relevance. Yesterday there was a bodyful of sensations, a head stuffed with thoughts, a world of fate and action beyond one's skin and disarticulated rhythms and nonrhythms jangling and jagging within. Then there's inexplicably a congealing, a gathering of still inchoate purposes, and an instantaneous awareness of what's to come as the poem receives or gives its shape to its experience. Then one learns where he's been by getting there. This is where I find I'd been in "1956."

David Ettlman

Denise Levertov

THE GODDESS

She in whose lipservice
I passed my time,
whose name I knew, but not her face,
came upon me where I lay in Lie Castle!

Flung me across the room, and
room after room (hitting the wall, re-
bounding—to the last
sticky wall—wrenching away from it
pulled hair out!)
till I lay
outside the outer walls!

There in cold air
lying still where her hand had thrown me,
I tasted the mud that splattered my lips:
the seeds of a forest were in it,
asleep and growing! I tasted
her power!

The silence was answering my silence,
a forest was pushing itself
out of sleep between my submerged fingers.

I bit on a seed and it spoke on my tongue
of day that shone already among stars
in the water-mirror of low ground,

and a wind rising ruffled the lights:
she passed near me returning from the encounter,
she who plucked me from the close rooms,

without whom nothing
flowers, fruits, sleeps in season,
without whom nothing
speaks in its own tongue, but returns
lie for lie!

I believe that poems should so arise from the sequence of the poet's experience that their relation to each other in the pattern of that experience makes it impossible for him to think, or to wish to think, of "a single favorite poem." One may feel—and one most often feels this way about one's most recent poem—that in one poem rather than another one has said more and said it more precisely; but these are superficial and fluctuating fondnesses. At a deeper level one can no more favor one poem—one part, that is, of the larger poem that is a lifetime's work-in-progress—than one can isolate other elements and events of a life for preference: they tend toward a whole, but as one cannot see the design till it is done, one cannot know the value of the parts or comprehend their interrelations except as time passes. Perhaps one might say that the right to choose a favorite among one's own poems is a privilege of old age; or that only in old age does it truly become a possibility. Similarly, the reader who serious- ly studies a poet's works will find it more difficult to "prefer" the deeper his studies take him; even though he may make critical evaluations, technical distinctions, he will find himself led to accept, eventually, even those works that at first, before he came to know the whole work, seemed irrelevant, or unattractive to his "taste"— because "taste" comes to seem a false, a superficial and pretentious, way of approach, itself irrelevant to the irreducible aliveness of a poem.

Nevertheless, I have chosen a poem not quite at random. I have chosen it because it is one that recalls to me one of those confrontations with Truth that every person, every soul, must sometimes experience if he or she is to live, to grow; and especially one who is a poet—for poets have a genius for lying and an adoration for the truth, and it may be that the driving impulse of every poet is to maintain the dynamic interplay of these two passions.

Denise Levertov

William H. Matchett

WATER OUZEL

For Dora Willson

Follow back from the gull's bright arc and the osprey's plunge,
Past the silent heron, erect in the tidal marsh,
Up the mighty river, rolling in mud. Branch off
At the sign of the kingfisher poised on a twisted snag.
Not deceived when the surface grows calm, keep on,
Past the placidity of ducks, the delusive pastoral dreams
Drawn down by the effortless swallows that drink on the wing.
With the wheat fields behind you, do not neglect to choose
At every juncture the clearest and coldest path.
Push through the reeds where the redwing sways,
Climb through the warnings of hidden jays,
Climb, climb the jostling, narrowing stream
Through aspen sunlight into the evergreen darkness
Where chattering crossbills scatter the shreds of cones.
Here at last at the brink of the furthest fall,
With the water dissolving to mist as it shatters the pool below,
Pause beneath timber-line springs and the melting snow.
Here, where the shadows are deep in the crystal air,
So near a myriad beginnings, after so long a journey,
Expecting at least a golden cockatoo
Or a screaming eagle with wings of flame,
Stifle your disappointment, observe
The burgher of all this beauty, the drab
Citizen of the headwaters; struggle to love
The ridiculous ouzel, perched on his slippery stone

Like an awkward, overblown catbird deprived of its tail.
Not for him the limitless soaring above the storm,
Or the surface-skimming, or swimming, or plunging in.
He walks. In the midst of the turbulence, bathed in spray,
From a rock without foothold into the lunging current
He descends a deliberate step at a time till, submerged,
He has walked from sight and hope. The stream
Drives on, dashes, splashes, drops over the edge,
Too swift for ice in midwinter, too cold
For life in midsummer, depositing any debris,
Leaf, twig or carcass, along the way,
Wedging them in behind rocks to rot,
Such as these not reaching the ocean.

Yet, lo, the lost one emerges unharmed,
Hardly wet as he walks from the water.
Undisturbed by beauty or terror, pursuing
His own few needs with a nerveless will,
Nonchalant in the torrent, he bobs and nods
As though to acknowledge implicit applause.
This ceaseless tic, a trick of the muscles shared
With the solitary sandpiper, burlesqued
By the teeter-bob and the phoebe's tail,
Is not related to approbation. The dipper,
Denied the adventure of uncharted flight
Over vast waters to an unknown homeland, denied
Bodily beauty, slightly absurd and eccentric,
Will never attain acclaim as a popular hero.
No prize committee selects the clown
Whose only dangers are daily and domestic.

Yet he persists, and does not consider it persisting.
On a starless, sub-zero, northern night,

When all else has taken flight into sleep or the south,
He, on the edge of the stream, has been heard to repeat
The rippling notes of his song, which are clear and sweet.

"Water Ouzel" is an affirmation, a discovery of joy at the core of things, in spite of appearances and limitations. After the poem had been around for a while, I began to fear that it might be soft: it was not the whole story. Therefore I undertook "The Petrel," a complementary discovery of evil at the core of things. I don't understand either the goodness or the evil, but they are both there. Perhaps I am moved more deeply by the unexpected goodness; at any rate, I still prefer "Water Ouzel." A poem need not be all-inclusive; it need only realize a possible human experience. Nor do I now think the poem is soft. It insists upon the limits. Otherwise there would be no surprise.

The poem was not originally written for Dora Willson, but I gave it to her when we learned that she was dying. There seemed no adequate way to thank her for shared insight. There was nothing drab or ridiculous about Dora—the dedication does not make the poem an allegory—but she did live close to the sources, and she lived there with courage and joy.

William H. Matchett

Louis Simpson

WALT WHITMAN AT BEAR MOUNTAIN

. . . life which does not give the preference to any other life,
of any previous period, which therefore prefers its own exist-
ence . . .
Ortega y Gasset

Neither on horseback nor seated,
But like himself, squarely on two feet,
The poet of death and lilacs
Loafs by the footpath. Even the bronze looks alive
Where it is folded like cloth. And he seems friendly.

"Where is the Mississippi panorama
And the girl who played the piano?
Where are you, Walt?
The Open Road goes to the used-car lot.

"Where is the nation you promised?
These houses built of wood sustain
Colossal snows,
And the light above the street is sick to death.

"As for the people—see how they neglect you!
Only a poet pauses to read the inscription."

"I am here," he answered.
"It seems you have found me out.
Yet, did I not warn you that it was Myself
I advertised? Were my words not sufficiently plain?

"I gave no prescriptions,
And those who have taken my moods for prophecies
Mistake the matter."
Then, vastly amused—"Why do you reproach me?
I freely confess I am wholly disreputable.
Yet I am happy, because you have found me out."

A crocodile in wrinkled metal loafing . . .

Then all the realtors,
Pickpockets, salesmen, and the actors performing
Official scenarios,
Turned a deaf ear, for they had contracted
American dreams.

But the man who keeps a store on a lonely road,
And the housewife who knows she's dumb,
And the earth, are relieved.

All that grave weight of America
Cancelled! Like Greece and Rome.
The future in ruins!
The castles, the prisons, the cathedrals
Unbuilding, and roses
Blossoming from the stones that are not there . . .

The clouds are lifting from the high Sierras.
The Bay mists clearing;
And the angel in the gate, the flowering plum,
Dances like Italy, imagining red.

I have chosen to be represented by "Walt Whitman at Bear Mountain"—not because I think it the best poem I have written, but because it marked a turning-point in my work. I had recently published a book of poems, *A Dream of Governors*, in which I had solved to my satisfaction certain difficulties of writing "in form"—that is, in regular meter and rhyme. But now I felt that my skill was a strait-jacket. Also, inevitably, the adoption of traditional forms led me into a certain way of ending a poem, polishing it off, so to speak, that sometimes distorted my real meaning. It was time, I felt, to write a new kind of poem. I wanted to write a poem that would be less "willed." I would let images speak for themselves. The poem would be a statement, of course—there really is no such thing as a poem of pure metaphor or image—but I wanted the statement to be determined by the poem itself, to let my original feeling develop, without confining it in any strict fashion.

Of course, this was a matter of degree. Even the poem that seems most free is confined in some way—if by nothing more evident than the limitations of the poet's subconscious. What I did manage to arrive at in "Walt Whitman" was a poem that presented certain images and ideas in an almost colloquial manner, in lines whose rhythm was determined by my own habits of speech. This was not absolute freedom, but the result was more satisfying to me than recent poems in which I had presented ideas in neat rhymes. In fact, whatever theory about the writing of verse enables a poet to speak the truth and fills him with energy, is good. My groping toward a poetry of significant images and spoken lines enabled me to say certain things that I had not been able to say before. This poem was followed by others in which I was able to deal with material that interested me—poems about history, my own personal life, America.

"Walt Whitman at Bear Mountain" springs from an actual experience, as do most of my poems. About three years ago I traveled up the Hudson River to Bear Mountain with my wife and the poet Robert Bly and his wife. We came upon the Jo Davidson (I believe that's the right spelling) statue of Walt Whitman. The statue was very impressive under the leaves. A few days later I started this poem. I didn't finish it for months, not until I had moved to California. The fragments of what I had attempted then cohered all at once—this is the way it happens with me, if I'm lucky.

Whitman means a great deal to me. When I came to America, at the age of seventeen, an intelligent cousin gave me a copy of *Leaves of Grass*. I recognized immediately that Whitman was a great, original poet. I now think that he is the greatest poet we have had in America. But I think that most of his prophecies have been proved wrong. It is a strange fact, when you think about it—that a poet can be great and yet be mistaken in his ideas. The Whitman who heralds an inevitable march of Democracy, who praises the intelligence of the masses, is nearly always mistaken. At least, if there ever was an America like that, it no longer exists. But the Whitman who uses his own eyes and ears, who describes things, who expresses his own sly humor or pathos, is unbeatable. I tried to show the two Whitmans in my poem. I used my ideas about Whitman as a way of getting at my own ideas about America. And I think a great deal about the country I live in; indeed, it seems an inexhaustible subject, one that has hardly been tapped. By America, I mean the infinitely complex life we have. Sometimes when I look at Main Street, I feel like a stranger looking at the Via Aurelia, or the Pyramids. But our monuments are ephemeral. Poetry is the art of the ephemeral.

It is hard to talk about a poem, for talking about poetry leads you out in every direction. I do not see the art of poetry as separated from life.

Louis Simpson

Edgar Bowers

TWO POEMS
ON THE CATHOLIC
BAVARIANS

1
The fierce and brooding holocaust of faith
This people conquered, which no edict could,
And wove its spirit stiff and rich like cloth
That many years ago was soaked in blood.

Their minds are active only in their hands
To check and take the labor of the hills,
To furnish nature its precise demands
And bear its harshness as it seems God wills.

But holy passion hurts them in each season
To blend themselves with nature if they can;
They find in well known change enough of reason
To worship Him in it as Him in Man.

Thus in the summer on the Alpine heights
A deity of senseless wrath and scorn
Is feasted through the equinoctial nights
As though a savage Christ were then reborn.

Up from the floors of churches in December
The passion rises to a turbulence
Of darkness such as threatens to dismember
The mind submerged in bestial innocence.

And Druid shades with old dementia fraught
Possess the souls they had accounted loss
And join their voices, raging and distraught,
About the curious symbol of the cross.

2
I know a wasted place high in the Alps
Called Witches's Kitchen. There the sun all day
With aberrant change of shadows plagues the eyes,
And when the equinoctial moon has play

Upon the beast-like monoliths of stone,
The blood runs cold as its old passions rise
To haunt the memory of what we are
And what we do in worshipping brute skies.

Below this waste of spirit and of mind
The village Holy Blood with ordered care
Was founded on deep meadows. Yearly, sheep
Are brought to graze in summer pastures there.

Its people sow and harvest grain together
Between the comings of the winter's ice,
And when they stop to take a quick sprung flower,
Its being and their gesture will suffice

To balance what they are and what are not.
And if we turn to look within the town
Upon a wall we find the stencilled group
Of Mary, John and others taking down

The body of their Master from the tree.
And just at dusk the daylight's weakened pace
Shades the blue chalk of Mary's robe with red;
And her faint tears are red upon His face.

I have chosen this poem partly because, though it is one of my poems which I like best, no one has seen fit to include it in an anthology. My other reason is that it is one of the very earliest of my poems which seems to me successful still. In it, I think I was able to master the method I was trying to master at the time, late in 1947 and early in 1948. The method is, simply, to develop a logical analysis by means of and in terms of statements about and descriptions of things, scenes, and events. Here I think I was able to realize my two-fold purpose rather well, the purpose being to make the descriptions good in themselves and, at the same time, to give them significance, both of wit and feeling. Therefore, the poem must have been a proof that I could do what I wished to do and an encouragement to continue trying.

Edgar Bowers

Michael Hamburger

SECURITY

1

So he's got there at last, been received as a partner—
In a firm going bankrupt;
Found the right place (walled garden), arranged for a mort-
gage—
But they're pulling the house down
To make room for traffic.

Worse winds are rising. He takes out new policies
For his furniture, for his life,
At a higher premium
Against more limited risks.

2

Who can face the winds, till the panes crack in their frames?
And if a man faced them, what in the end could he do
But look for shelter like all the rest?
The winds too are afraid, and blow from fear.

3

I hear my children at play
And recall that one branch of the elm-tree looks dead;
Also that twenty years ago now I could have been parchment
Cured and stretched for a lampshade,
Who now have children, a lampshade
And the fear of those winds.

I saw off the elm-tree branch
To find that the wood was sound;
Mend the fences yet again,
Knowing they'll keep out no one,
Let alone the winds.
For still my children play
And shall tomorrow, if the weather holds.

This is a recent poem, only a few months old, perhaps too recent for me to be sure about. I choose it here for entirely personal reasons. Partly because it was easy to write, because it was one of three poems written in as many days—all of them unexpected and unprepared. For many years I had written slowly, taking most poems through draft after draft, sometimes abandoning them to take them up again months or years later—or not at all. Something was wrong; and it was those three poems that told me what was wrong. I was brought up on the notion of the impersonality of art, and had taken the "objective correlative" too much to heart. This meant that I wrote too formally, distilled experience till it seemed not mine but anyone's—or no one's, and became what people call a "literary" poet.

It took me a long time to understand why my best poems were often those that I took least seriously: they were least laboured. "Security" broke down the specious division I had made in my mind between serious and light verse. It was written in the casual manner I had reserved for epigrams and occasional pieces; it was not a correlative of private experience, not a symbolic distillation of it, but a free mixture of immediate and imagined experience. Metrically and rhythmically, too, it was free. I am grateful to and for this poem because I find I can go on from it to where I now know I should have gone long ago. If I've written better poems, they don't concern me at present because I'm not going their way.

Michael Hamburger

225

Vassar Miller

THE ONE THING NEEDFUL

"The cause of loving God is God alone
And measure of this love there should be none,"
Lest Bernard take my riming him amiss,
I'll tell him there's no poetry but this.

Therefore, young priest, as good as debonair,
Who give your gospel with so fine a flare,
I'd not quarrel with you on a single phrase
Save to remind you what St. Bernard says,

And more, "The Love that saved us from damnation
Saved angels from the need of such salvation."
Have you, I wonder, ever understood
Love so impartial perils platitude?

You witness that since first you yielded up
Your all to God, he's overflowed your cup.
You give, God gives—so far a game God's won.
Who, after all, outplays the Champion?

I do not hint you'd not serve God for nought,
Nor from the malice whetted on such thought
Give theologians room to theorize
That Satan is a sorehead in disguise.

I'm certain that your grief-astounded gaze,
Adjusting, would dissolve to tears of praise.
For so did Francis's in rapt communions,
St. Joan of Arc's, blunt Luther's, and poor Bunyon's.

And Job himself, though he could not approve
God's justice, could do nothing else but love
As he could not help breathing, being hungry
For air, no less so when the air turned angry.

But still the love we have no right to measure
Concerns itself with neither pain nor pleasure.
What then? St. Bernard tells us. And there is,
God knows, no rime nor reason except his.

I wrote "The One Thing Needful" in love and anger. I used to say
that a poem is an act of love. Now I know that it is an act of hate also.
At best, these two emotions are not mutually exclusive.

Vassar Miller

Donald Justice

AFTER A LINE BY
JOHN PEALE BISHOP

Why will they never speak,
The old ones, the grandfathers?
Always you find them sitting
On ruined porches, deep
In the back country, at dusk,
Hawking and spitting.
They might have sat there forever,
Tapping their sticks,
Peevish, discredited gods.
Ask of the traveler how
At road-end they will fix
You maybe with the cold
Eye of a snake or a bird
And answer not a word,
Only these dark, oracular
Head-shakes or head-nods.

The line from Bishop is the first line of his "Ode" about the Fates:
"Why will they never sleep?" I remembered how in their old age my
grandfathers, retired farmers, used to sit on their porches for hours
with nothing to do and, if you asked too many questions, nothing
to say. Fine men; but mysterious, a little terrifying to a child. They

were like those old men in the backwoods of whom you have to ask directions when you are lost, hard to get satisfaction from. A little like the stone gods you might come on in some Eastern jungle— whose silence is absolute. If, as it happens, I like this poem better than my friends seem to, it must be because of what I tried to bring together in it; or maybe only because of what I was unable to get in, those other intended stanzas of variation on Bishop's line—the child at his grandfather's feet, the look of the fields when you are lost.

Donald Justice

John Wain

POEM

Hippolytus: *Do you see my plight, Queen, stricken as I am?*
Artemis: *I see. But my eyes are not permitted to shed tears.*
Euripides, *Hippolytus,* 1395-96.

Like a deaf man meshed in his endless silence
the earth goes swishing through the heavens' wideness.

Doubtless some god with benign inquiring brow
could lean over and let his brown eye so true

play over its whirling scabby hide with a look of searching
till suddenly, with eye and bland forefinger converging

he points to a specially found spot. *Here, this moment*
he might say, *I detect it; this is the locus of torment:*

This spot is the saddest on the earth's entire crust.
A quaint fancy? Such gods can scarcely exist?

Still, the fact outlives the metaphor it breeds;
whether or not the god exists, the scored earth bleeds.

There must be a point where pain takes its worst hold.
One spot, somewhere, holds the worst grief in the world.

Who would venture a guess as to where this grief lies cupped?
Ah, from minute to minute it could never be mapped.

For trouble flies between molecules like a dream.
It flowers from the snapped edge of bones like sour flame.

Who knows what child lies in a night like a mine-shaft
unblinking, his world like a fallen apple mashed and cleft?

Or what failed saint plummets into his private chasm
having bartered all Heaven for one stifling orgasm?

Or perhaps it is even an animal who suffers worst,
gentle furry bundle or two-headed obscene pest.

But where pain's purest drop burns deep no one could say,
unless it were this god with benign brown eye.

Some would curse this god for doing nothing to help.
But he has knowledge like cold water on his scalp.

To perceive that spirit of suffering in its raging purity
is to a god the burden of his divinity.

O then, if he exists, have pity on this god.
He is clamped to that wounded crust with its slime of blood.

He has no ignorance to hold him separate.
Everything is known to a god. The gods are desperate.

I had to puzzle for a long time before I arrived at a choice for this
anthology. I couldn't pick a favourite poem because I don't have
favourites among my own poems: this sounds priggish or even false,
but what I mean is that my poems stand in a quite different relation-

ship to me, their author, from that of my other writings. If I write a novel, or a story, or a critical essay, I soon make up my mind as to its merits; I can read it, more or less, as if it had been written by someone else. But I cannot do this with my poems because they are more instinctual; they arrive, from some deep place in my being where forces are at work which I cannot command, though I can thwart and deny them. After a poem has arrived, and been born, I look at it much as one looks at a natural object: I didn't *write* it— it happened to me. As a professional writer, I can say, "To-day I will write a story," or some criticism, or a scene for a play, or whatever it may be: but I cannot say, and no one has ever been able to say, "To-day I will write poetry."

It follows that when I have assembled a sheaf of these events in my life which I call poems, I never make any attempt to discriminate among them. I find myself, instead, taking the word of other people. I may dislike one of my poems, but if one or two people say, unprompted, that they like it, then the next time I am making a collection to go into a book, in it goes. If it has spoken to someone else, it has proved itself. Whatever the impulse that caused those words to come out in that order, it has turned out to be an impulse that can re-create itself, by means of those words, in another mind, a mind independent of my own. And that, for me, settles the matter. For this reason I can hardly imagine myself, in later life, issuing "Collected" volumes in which I prune, polish and generally "improve" the work of my younger poetic self. A clumsy line here or there, perhaps, I may straighten out; an unconscious plagiarism I may remove, if only in deference to the poet plagiarised; but a radical reworking I cannot imagine, since if I were in the mood to be working on poetry I should be writing another poem.

So when I cast about for a poem to go into this selection, I finally lit on one of the few whose occasion I happen to remember and of whose genesis I can, therefore, give a clear (though not a complete) account. One evening in 1957 I was sitting alone in my flat, reading a newspaper, when I came upon a short news item, down at the bottom of a column, that seemed to me infinitely pathetic. I have forgotten the exact wording and most of the details, but the gist of it was that a small group of Italian soldiers, a dozen or so, had, by some strange quirk of military history, been taken prisoner by the Russians during the Second World War. None of these men had ever been heard of again, but one day—and this was the occasion of the news paragraph I was reading—a pigeon had been brought down, somewhere or other, with a piece of paper tied to its leg, bearing the desperate scrawled message that these Italians were engaged in slave labour somewhere in the Arctic Circle, and had been ever since 1945, and that they appealed to whoever found the pigeon's note to try to do something for them.

Sitting by my electric fire, the newspaper in my hand, I tried to put myself, imaginatively, in the place of these captives. But to be in their place, even imaginatively, was so horrible that I soon gave it up, and my mind turned, almost with relief, to thinking along more general lines. The sheer concentration of human misery in the hut where the Italians were kept: the desperate whispered conversations; the incredible patience that must have gone into snaring the pigeon and managing to get it away with the note tied to its leg, without being seen by the guards; their emotions as the bird flew away out of sight: finally, the numbing certainty that nothing could be done for them. Their crime, which was simply to be conscripted into the army of their country, was to be punished without end; nothing lay before them but misery and death. I tried to imagine a suffering worse than theirs: if I couldn't, did this mean that the spot which contained them was the unhappiest spot on the earth's surface? Then the thought broke in on me that, quite probably, the deepest and most inconsolable grief in the world, if only one could know where it was, might have nothing to do with political persecution, slavery or any cruelty inflicted from outside. At this thought, the poem began to move inside me, and within half an hour I had it written in the form in which it is printed here. The epigraph from Euripides was added later, when it became plain that the poem had naturally moved, or wandered, towards the subject of a possible divinity and its nature.

John Wain

Elizabeth Jennings

FOUNTAIN

Let it disturb no more at first
Than the hint of a pool predicted far in a forest,
Or a sea so far away that you have to open
Your window to hear it.
Think of it then as elemental, as being
Necessity,
Not for a cup to be taken to it and not
For lips to linger or eye to receive itself
Back in reflection, simply
As water the patient moon persuades and stirs.

And then step closer,
Imagine rivers you might indeed embark on,
Waterfalls where you could
Silence an afternoon by staring but never
See the same tumult twice.
Yes come out of the narrow street and enter
The full piazza. Come where the noise compels.
Statues are bowing down to the breaking air.

Observe it there—the fountain, too fast for shadows,
Too wild for the lights which illuminate it to hold,
Even a moment, an ounce of water back;
Stare at such prodigality and consider
It is the elegance here, it is the taming,

The keeping fast in a thousand flowering sprays,
That builds this energy up but lets the watchers
See in that stress an image of utter calm,
A stillness there. It is how we must have felt
Once at the edge of some perpetual stream,
Fearful of touching, bringing no thirst at all,
Panicked by no perception of ourselves
But drawing the water down to the deepest wonder.

This poem is about power or, more precisely, about the power which lies behind energy held in check. The poem was written in Rome in 1957 when my eyes had been glutted with the size and shape and ingenuity of countless fountains. Yet the poem was not about any particular fountain; rather, it was concerned with an idea which had obsessed me for several years—the enormous power of controlled strength—but had never before found the proper context for. I had written a number of poems about power and its many aspects, but none of them had wholly pleased me. It is perhaps ironic, as well as of some literary interest, that when I did at last find the medium, the music, the image for my idea, I was not directly searching for it.

"Fountain" was written at great speed and with a sense of ease and delight. Indeed, I find that all my poems which I continue to like have been written very quickly and with a strong feeling of rightness and concentration. I revise poems very little, though I destroy a great many. My notebooks are filled with stillborn ones and with odd sentences and half-sentences.

Though I value very highly the intellectual quality of a poem, the making of poems has for me something of the feeling of being possessed. One can discipline oneself and make experiments, yes, but finally the poem is given, not sought out. "Fountain" makes a statement but it is one of my own favourite poems because the idea which it expresses seems to be completely at one with the sensuous image.

236

I also hope that it communicates something, and I myself would certainly rather let my poems speak for themselves than write about them. I am not afraid of the inquiries of literary critics but I do believe that the poet can harm himself by tampering with and questioning his own creative energy too much. Making poems is not a religion but I believe that it has something in common with religious experience. For me, it is a major preoccupation.

Elizabeth Jennings

James Merrill

THE COUNTRY OF A THOUSAND YEARS OF PEACE

Here they all come to die,
Fluent therein as in a fourth tongue.
But for a young man not yet of their race
It was madness you should lie

Blind in one eye, and fed
By the blood of a scrubbed face;
It was madness to look down
On the toy city where

The glittering neutrality
Of clock and chocolate and lake and cloud
Made every morning somewhat
Less than you could bear;

And makes me cry aloud
At the old masters of disease
Who dangling high about you on a hair
The sword that, never falling, kills

Would coax you still back from that starry land
Under the world, which no one sees
Without a death, its finish and sharp weight
Flashing in his own hand.

In 1950, at the beginning of nearly three years abroad, I went to Lausanne for an hour with my friend the Dutch poet Hans Lodeizen. He had been reading George Sand's autobiography; there was Roussel on the phonograph and a Picasso etching of acrobats on the floor. The June sunset filled up his hospital room. He spoke with carefree relish of the injection they would give him presently. Before I left we agreed to meet in Italy sometime that fall. He had leukemia and died two weeks later, at twenty-six. It was my first deeply-felt death. I connected it with the spell of aimless living in Europe to which I was then committed and to which all those picturesque and novel sights corresponded painfully enough. As the inevitable verses took shape, strictness of form seemed at last beside the point; my material nevertheless allowed for a good deal of paring and polishing. Eight years later, a word from Barbara Deming led me to rephrase the last four lines; another, from Benjamin DeMott, to make use of the second person. The poem still surprises me, as much by its clarification of what I was feeling, as by its foreknowledge of where I needed to go next, in my work.

James Merrill

Alastair Reid

A GAME OF GLASS

I do not believe this room
with its cat and its chandelier,
its chessboard-tiled floor,
and its shutters that open out
on an angel playing a fountain,
and the striped light slivering in
to a room that looks the same
in the mirror over my shoulder,
with a second glass-eyed cat.

My book does not look real.
The room and the mirror seem
to be playing a waiting game.
The cat has made its move,
the fountain has one to play,
and the thousand eyes of the angel
in the chandelier above
gleam beadily, and say
the next move is up to me.

How can I trust my luck?
Whatever way I look,
I cannot tell which is the door,
and I do not know who is who—
the thin man in the mirror,

or the watery one in the fountain.
The cat is eyeing my book.
What am I meant to do?
Which side is the mirror on?

"A Game of Glass" is the one poem of mine which *occurred* to me, as an actual happening—the only thing I had to do was to catch it and hold it in words as clearly as possible.

I was sitting in my workroom in Spain, one morning very early, writing. The room was exactly as reconstituted in the poem—a large mirror on the wall behind me, shutters in front of me opening to the fountained garden, a huge chandelier, a black and white tiled floor, and my writing table in the middle. All at once, I looked up, and caught the eyes of the cat gazing at me intently—and I felt, for an endless moment, a realisation of utter mystery, in which I existed in no familiar sense, but was simply one element in a vast, inexplicable game, which the cat understood more completely than I. There was something of Through the Looking Glass about it; the feeling was awesome. The coinciding reflections, the chessboard, the un-recognition, all sustained the moment; the poem followed almost at once. I cannot be sure that my profound astonishment is properly contained in it; but I do know that whenever I happen to read it over, I re-enter the moment most vividly, as more than a memory.

Except in the manner of its happening, the poem is not out of key with the rest of my work, since to explore the amazement of finding myself alive has been my preoccupation. But this poem reassures me; through it, I can feel beyond words to the happening itself, and real-ise always that the mystery *does* exist, prior to them.

Alastair Reid

W. D. Snodgrass

A FLAT ONE

Old Fritz, on this rotating bed
For seven wasted months you lay
Unfit to move, shrunken, gray,
No good to yourself or anyone
But to be babied—changed and bathed and fed.
      At long last, that's all done.

Before each meal, twice every night,
We set pads on your bedsores, shut
Your catheter tube off, then brought
The second canvas-and-black-iron
Bedframe and clamped you in between them, tight,
      Scared, so we could turn

You over. We washed you, covered you,
Cut up each bite of meat you ate;
We watched your lean jaws masticate
As ravenously your useless food
As thieves at hard labor in their chains chew
      Or insects in the wood.

Such pious sacrifice to give
You all you could demand of pain:
Receive this haddock's body, slain

For you, old tyrant; take this blood
Of a tomato, shed that you might live.
　　　　You had that costly food.

　　You seem to be all finished, so
　　We'll plug your old recalcitrant anus
　　And tie up your discouraged penis
　　In a great, snow-white bow of gauze.
We wrap you, pin you, and cart you down below,
　　　　Below, below, because

　　Your credit has finally run out.
　　On our steel table, trussed and carved,
　　You'll find this world's hardworking, starved
　　Teeth working in your precious skin.
The earth turns, in the end, by turn about
　　　　And opens to take you in.

　　Seven months gone down the drain; thank God
　　That's through. Throw out the four-by-fours,
　　Swagsticks, the thick salve for bedsores,
　　Throw out the diaper pads and drug
Containers, pile the bedclothes in a wad,
　　　　And rinse the cider jug

　　Half filled with the last urine. Then
　　Empty out the cotton cans,
　　Autoclave the bowls and spit pans,
　　Unhook the pumps and all the red
Tubes—catheter, suction, oxygen;
　　　　Next, wash the empty bed.

—All this Dark Age machinery
On which we had tormented you
To life. Last, we collect the few
Belongings: snapshots, some odd bills,
Your mail, and half a pack of Luckies we
   Won't light you after meals.

  Old man, these seven months you've lain
  Determined—not that you would live—
  Just not to die. No one would give
  You one chance you could ever wake
From that first night, much less go well again,
   Much less go home and make

  Your living; how could you hope to find
  A place for yourself in all creation?—
  Pain was your only occupation.
  And pain that should content and will
A man to give it up, nerved you to grind
   Your clenched teeth, breathing, till

  Your skin broke down, your calves went flat
  And your legs lost all sensation. Still,
  You took enough morphine to kill
  A strong man. Finally, nitrogen
Mustard: you could last two months after that;
   It would kill you then.

  Even then you wouldn't quit.
  Old soldier, yet you must have known
  Inside the animal had grown

Sick of the world, made up its mind
To stop. Your mind ground on its separate
                Way, merciless and blind,

        Into these last weeks when the breath
        Would only come in fits and starts
        That puffed out your sections like the parts
        Of some enormous, damaged bug.
You waited, not for life, not for your death,
                Just for the deadening drug

        That made your life seem bearable.
        You still whispered you would not die.
        Yet in the nights I heard you cry
        Like a whipped child; in fierce old age
You whimpered, tears stood on your gun-metal
                Blue cheeks shaking with rage

        And terror. So much pain would fill
        Your room that when I left I'd pray
        That if I came back the next day
        I'd find you gone. You stayed for me—
Nailed to your own rapacious, stiff self-will.
                You've shook loose, finally.

        They'd say this was a worthwhile job
        Unless they tried it. It is mad
        To throw our good lives after bad;
                Waste time, drugs, and our minds, while strong
Men starve. How many young men did we rob
                To keep you hanging on?

I can't think we did *you* much good.
Well, when you died, none of us wept.
You killed for us, and so we kept
You, because we need to earn *our* pay.
No. We'd still have to help you try. We would
Have killed for you today.

I picked this poem for several reasons. First, I enjoy reading it to audiences; it moves and upsets them. Besides, a number of my friends have liked it, which relieves and encourages me. Again, I am personally glad to have gotten into a poem, whether successful or not, a problem and a set of details (catheters, Foster Frame beds, autoclaves, etc.) which hadn't been there before so far as I know.

But I suppose I most like this poem because it cost me so much work and I think I have now attacked the problems in it which for a long time I feared would completely defeat me. I wrote its first version as an assignment for John Berryman's poetry workshop at the State University of Iowa. That version, to my shock, was printed in *New World Writing;* I thought it promising, but scarcely finished. It was full of undigested chunks of that metaphysical-symbolist style we had been taught there—fancy rhetoric and heavy symbology. Like the hieratic symbolist poem, too, its emotions were scrambled, balanced, static. Again, the symbolist style always encouraged my desire to see all problems as intellectual and moral, ignoring the personal, emotional and dramatic. These were the tendencies I had been fighting, for I now wanted a poetry worldly, secular, changing, dramatic.

It took me six or eight years to see what was wrong with that version. Then I had to go back and sort out the poem's emotions—push all the angry emotions toward the beginning, and the sympathetic or resigned emotions toward the ending. This gave me much more the sort of poem, involving movement and change-of-mind, which I wanted. But as usual, I could not dramatize that change-of-mind without giving my speaker an action: he had to indulge himself in that orgy of scrubbing-up and throwing-out, before he could come to recognize his own sympathy with the dead man. That gave me a poem almost twice as long and surely quite different in the kind of effect it hopes to achieve.

W. D. Snodgrass

David Wagoner

THE NESTING GROUND

Piping sharp as a reed,
The small bird stood its ground
Twenty feet from ours.
From the shore, another answered
(The piercing double note
Meant killdeer and killdeer)
And skimmed over the sand,
Over the sparse grass,
Lit, then scurried away,
Flopping, crooking its wing
To flash a jagged streak
And the amber of its back.

When the first bird moved a foot
And struck out at the air,
Two chicks leaped after it,
Their plain heads clear as day.
We walked straight to the spot,
Needing to stir what we love,
Knelt down and found nothing,
Not even when we stared
Each checkered, pebbly stalk
Into its own semblance.
We flattened disbelief
With the four palms of our hands.

But the grown birds broke themselves,
Crippled their cries and wings
So near us, we stood up
To follow their sacrifice
That tempts the nails of creatures
Who, needing flight, forget
Whatever they might have caught
By standing still instead.
We kept on walking, led
By pretended injuries,
Till we were far away,
Then turned, as the birds turned
To sail back to the source
Where we had touched our knees,
And saw through our strongest glass
The young spring out of cover,
Piping one death was over.

The poems I most admire are simultaneously free and controlled; they have no padding, yet aren't jammed together; the lines tend to be "open" most of the time, without knotted syntax, or metaphors at cross-purposes visually. The rhythm is related to the subject matter and doesn't simply drone. The poems tend to be dramatic presentations which have to account for themselves with as little author comment as possible. (I admire, but from a distance, poets whose sole method is learned discourse, alternately acid and gabby.) I dislike poets that swarm around their matter, become too insistent, never seem sure what they have already accomplished but must do it again and again, like a lesser Victorian who has discovered a spring flower and treats it like an all-day sucker. Finally, I most admire poems which have unearthed something of genuine value to the poet himself and, therefore, to anyone willing to go along with him: the symptoms are hard to name, but they persuade me. In all these terms and at this particular time, late 1961, "The Nesting Ground" is, for me, one of my least disappointing poems.

David Wagoner

Henri Coulette

INTAGLIO

I have a picture in my room in which
Four gawky children strike a pose and stare
Out at the world without a worldly care.
Three girls and a boy in a paper hat:
The one too much a mouse to be a bitch,
The bitch, the actress, and the acrobat.

The roles I give them, half suggested by
The poses that they took, are meaningless,
For they are playing games. It is recess
Or summer—we have interrupted them.
They pose for us, with Agile romping by
And dark-eyed Pensive plucking at her hem.

This is my family. I dust them now
And then, and they return the courtesy
By never growing up. Thus, irony
Becomes a kind of family likeness, treasured
Not for the casual sameness of a brow
But for the attitudes one's mind has measured.

I knew an Agile once. To prove himself
The nimbler one, he pushed his books aside,
And crossed to Europe and the war, and died,

And his agility, which I believed a power
Then, then was gone, and his books on my shelf
Harvest the sunlit dust, hour after hour.

And there was Pensive, too, and everything
She touched was touched with fear. She married well,
Her people said, but marriage proves a hell
For those who marry but the flesh alone.
Who would have known a turn of mind could bring
Such knowledge to a girl? Who would have known?

I think of her, the child with heavy heart,
Heavy with child, and, Child, I think of you
And all the follies you will journey through;
I know them as an author knows his book.
Action and thought are nothing if apart.
Love in a gesture, wisdom in a look—

These are the real births for which we die.
Outside, the neighbor children startle me,
Calling, "Allee, alleoutsinfree."
They cut for home. I hear a whirring skate
Fading through the darkness like a sigh.
I dust the frame and set the picture straight.

They who appear here—my poor children in adult garb—are dead now. It pleases me to think, though, that they still live in these lines.

I wrote this poem in the fall of 1956. I hadn't written anything for a year, and I had yet to write a real poem. "Intaglio" started as an exercise, an attempt to catch something of the meter of Wyatt in "They Flee from Me." I had a print of Sylvia Petrie's "The

Land of Children" over my desk. Wouldn't a description of it serve for a subject? And wouldn't that please Sylvia? I began to look more closely at the faces in the print.

The exercise failed. But "Intaglio" had become my first real poem, and the children were to lead me to other poems.

Sylvia, I think, was pleased.

Henri Coulette

Galway Kinnell

THE SUPPER AFTER THE LAST

1
The desert moves out on half the horizon
Rimming the illusory water which, among islands,
Bears up the sky. The sea scumbles in
From its own inviolate border under the sky.
A dragon-fly floating on six legs on the sand
Lifts its green-yellow tail, declines its wings
A little, flutters them a little, and lays
On dazzled sand the shadow of its wings. Near shore
A bather wades through his shadow in the water.
He tramples and kicks it; it recomposes.

2
Outside the open door
Of the white-washed house,
Framed in its doorway, a chair,
Vacant, waits in the sunshine.

A jug of fresh water stands
Inside the door. In the sunshine
The chair waits, less and less vacant.
The host's plan is to offer water, then stand aside.

3

They eat *rosé* and chicken. The chicken head
Has been tucked under the shelter of the wing.
Beneath the table a red-backed, passionate dog
Cracks chicken bones on the blood and gravel floor.
No one else but the dog and the blind
Cat watching it knows who is that bearded
Wild man guzzling overhead, the wreck of passion
Emptying his eyes, who has not yet smiled,

Who stares at the company, where he is company,
Turns them to sacks of appalled, grinning skin,
Forks the fowl-eye out from under
The large, makeshift, cooked lid, evaporates the wine,

Jellies the sunlit table and spoons, floats
The deluxe grub down the intestines of the Styx,
Devours all but the cat and the dog, to whom he slips scraps,
The red-backed accomplice busy grinding gristle.

4

When the bones of the host
Crack in the hound's jaw
The wild man rises. Opening
His palms he announces:
I came not to astonish
But to destroy you. Your
Jug of cool water? Your
Hanker after wings? Your
Lech for transcendence?
I came to prove you are
Intricate and simple things

As you are, created
In the image of nothing,
Taught of the creator
By your images in dirt—

As mine, for which you set
A chair in the sunshine,
Mocking me with water!
As pictures of wings,
Not even iridescent,
That clasp the sand
And that cannot perish, you swear,
Having once been evoked!

5
The witnesses back off; the scene begins to float in water;
Far out in that mirage the Savior sits whispering to the world,
Becoming a mirage. The dog turns into a smear on the sand.
The cat grows taller and taller as it flees into space.

From the hot shine where he sits his whispering drifts:
You struggle from flesh into wings; the change exists.
But the wings that live gripping the contours of the dirt
Are all at once nothing, flesh and light lifted away.

You are the flesh; I am the resurrection, because I am the
    light.
I cut to your measure the creeping piece of darkness
That haunts you in the dirt. Step into light—
I make you over. I breed the shape of your grave in the dirt.

It is from this poem, "The Supper after the Last," that I want to make a fresh start, and I choose it for this reason. I mean towards a poem without scaffolding or occasion, that progresses through images to a point where it can make a statement on a major subject.

Galway Kinnell

W. S. Merwin

IN THE NIGHT FIELDS

I heard the sparrows shouting "Eat, eat,"
And then the day dragged its carcass in back of the hill.
Slowly the tracks darkened.

The smoke rose steadily from no fires.
The old hunger, left in the old darkness,
Turned like a hanged knife.
I would have preferred a quiet life.
The bugs of regret began their services
Using my spine as a rosary. I left the maps
For the spiders.
Let's go, I said.

                    Light of the heart,
The wheat had started lighting its lanterns,
And in every house in heaven there were lights waving
Hello good-bye. But that's
Another life.
Snug on the crumbling earth
The old bottles lay dreaming of new wine.
I picked up my breast, which had gone out.
By other lights I go looking for yours
Through the standing harvest of my lost arrows.
Under the moon the shadow

Practices mowing. Not for me, I say,
Please not for my
Benefit. A man cannot live by bread
Alone.

If I had to use one as an amulet I hope this one would serve.

W.S. Merwin

Charles Tomlinson

THE PICTURE OF J. T. IN A PROSPECT OF STONE

What should one
    wish a child
        and that, one's own,
emerging
    from between
            the stone lips
of a sheep-stile that divides
    village graves
          and village green?
—wish her
    the constancy of stone.
          —But stone
is hard.
    —Say, rather,
          it resists
the slow corrosives
    and the flight
          of time
and yet it takes
    the play, the fluency
          from light.
—How would you know
    the gift you'd give
          was the gift

she'd wish to have?
    —Gift is giving
             gift is meaning:
first
    I'd give
            then let her
live with it
    to prove
            its quality the better and
thus learn
    to love
            what (to begin with)
she might spurn.
    —You'd
            moralise a gift?
—I'd have her
    understand
            the gift I gave her.
—And so she shall
    but let her play
            her innocence away
emerging
    (as she does)
            between
her doom (unknown),
    her unmown green.

In this poem there has been an attempt to combine family associations with a moral climate and setting which yield up "the constancy of stone" as their fundamental image. The setting is the South West of England, in a district of Gloucestershire, where the buildings—

and even their roofs—are chiefly of stone. Here, there is one overriding experience—that of the continuity of stone architecture with both history and setting. A continuity, an ineradicable spirit of place, a land of limestone—"that humanistic rock," as Adrian Stokes calls it—all these seem to form for a poet a moral medium and a moral currency. What more natural than that he should try to unite these appearances, enriched by time, with that which is most youthful, most near and most fresh—a child of three, seen at play, as she is in the act of making use of them. Conceivably she will use them as spiritual tokens in the future—stone resting securely yet in disquality on unequal stone, buildings knit by common materials into locality—just as the poem uses them in which she appears, her passing presence qualified and judged by their durability. The mode of attention the poet hopes she gets is hinted at in his borrowing from Andrew Marvell's title, "The Picture of T. C. in a Prospect of Flowers." He chose the piece because it is perhaps more personal in tone than his other poems.

Charles Tomlinson

Phyllis Webb

MAKING

Quilted
patches, unlike the smooth slick loveliness
of the bought,
this made-ness out of self-madness
thrown across their bones to keep them warm.
It does.

Making
under the patches a smooth silk loveliness
of parts;
two bodies are better than one for this quilting,
throwing into the dark a this-ness that was not.
It does.

Fragments
of the splintered irrelevance of doubt, sharp
hopes, spear and splice into a nice consistency as once
under the pen, the brush, the sculptor's hand
music was made, arises now, blossom on fruit-tree bough.
It does.

Exercise
exegesis of the will captures and lays
haloes around bright ankles of a saint.
Exemplary under the tree,

Buddha glows out now
making the intolerable, accidental sky
patch up its fugitive ecstasies.
It does.

From the making made and, made, now making
certain order—thus excellent despair
is laid, and in the room the patches of the quilt
seize light and throw it back upon the air.
A grace is made, a loveliness is caught
quilting a quiet blossom as a work.
It does.

And do you,
doubting, fractured, and untaught, St. John of the Cross,
come down and patch the particles and throw
across the mild unblessedness of day
lectures to the untranscended soul.
Then lotus-like you'll move upon the pond,
the one-in-many, the many-in-the-one,
making a numbered floral-essenced sun
resting upon the greening padded frond,
a patched, matched protection for Because.
And for our dubious value it will do.
It always does.

I was surprised when this poem arrived with its "Quilted," but this, the patchwork quilt, was the given of the poem and became the central image controlling the range of ideas, keeping the concepts always in touch with the homely making.

I like the sound of this poem; I like the way "Making" travels its keyboard and shakes up the far end of the alphabet. After the first draft I immediately thought to cast it into a syllabic pattern based on the first stanza. But then I decided that the poem was already made: the rhythm was there, the oddness that seemed to me right, though I had not sought it, was there, and there was easiness too. For the poem simply happened on a May morning as I sat in the sun with my back against the wall.

It seems to me to be the answer to its companion piece, "Breaking," which had concluded with such awful tolerance, "What are we whole or beautiful or good for/but to be absolutely broken?" "Making" 's unhysterical, determined, open relativism is here both ethic and aesthetic. That's why I like the poem—because it says my centre.

William Dickey

LOVE AMONG THE MANICHEES

The blond cowl terse as a blunt threat to injure,
The claws instinctive to a triggering nerve,
I am a shut spring in my fanged disguises,
Aping the beast I serve.

I would be for you an offering of clear spirit,
Like water glistening over your spread hands,
Like the pattern described in air when the bird has left it,
Like not yet peopled lands.

Tick-laden fur ruffling for winds of danger,
I gorge on honey in the fallen tree,
Snarl at approachers to these laden acres
That bind their fruit to me.

I would be for you like a length of fallow
From the earliest world, like open mountainside
Too high for spurred seed to beat and follow,
For the edged wing to glide.

Puzzled, the shared beast lurks under my eyelids,
Dumb, menacing, not able to let go,
Or to conceive that who comes unconstrainéd
Stays the most easily so.

I would be for you as a willing mirror,
Plain crystal, undefined, of itself dumb,
That shapes its voice when you first look into it,
Smiling, "Now you have come."

"Love among the Manichees" remains one of my favorite poems, though it is some two years since it was written, for two reasons: first, that it seems as clear a statement as I ever got about a subject that has appeared in many of my poems; second, that it led me in directions of metrical technique which I've enjoyed following since.

The double nature of man—what Forster calls the beast and the monk—tried to get itself said often in poems I wrote, but this is the only place it seemed to me to come clear, without blurring at the edges. I suppose it is a question of discovering the locus in which the idea can finally act entirely, without being cumbered by fragments of other thoughts. Here, finally, the idea and the poem seemed to be co-extensive. Also, I thought the idea one important enough to be worth writing seriously about.

At the time the poem was written, I thought I was getting involved in facilely regular pentameters—the measure seemed to come out automatically. Here the metric isn't that regular, and the short final lines of the stanzas opened up possibilities which I've used in a lot of short-line poems since.

I like the poem because it has tried to be clear, to say something of high seriousness with as much simplicity, as much lucidity as I could manage to bring to the subject.

And I like it because it is a love poem. Though I like to write poems about all sorts of attitudes and concerns, there's a particular pleasure in saying something on the side of love.

Wm Dickey

Donald Hall

AN AIRSTRIP IN ESSEX

It is a lost road into the air.
It is a desert
among sugar beets.
The tiny wings
of the Spitfires of nineteen-forty-one
flake in the mud of the Channel.

Near the road a brick pillbox
totters under a load of grass,
where Home Guards waited
in the white fogs of the invasion winter.

Goodnight, old ruined war.

In Poland the wind rides on a jagged wall.
Smoke rises from the stones; no, it is mist.

I am fond of this poem because it took itself out of my hands. It moved not according to traditional symmetry but according to an unpredictable but necessary connection of particulars. I was writing at first about my feelings when I looked at the remains of a war.

Then I felt strangely that I must say goodbye to it, and my imagination turned to a greater suffering; and to a brief illusion of its endurance. I did not expect the leap which my poem took, but I came to value it more than anything I expected.

Donald Hall

Thomas Kinsella

ANOTHER SEPTEMBER

Dreams fled away, this country bedroom, raw
With the touch of the dawn, wrapped in a minor peace,
Hears through an open window the garden draw
Long pitch black breaths, lay bare its apple trees,
Ripe pear trees, brambles, windfall-sweetened soil,
Exhale rough sweetness against the starry slates.
Nearer the river sleeps St. John's, all toil
Locked fast inside a dream with iron gates.

Domestic Autumn, like an animal
Long used to handling by those countrymen,
Rubs her kind hide against the bedroom wall
Sensing a fragrant child come back again
—Not this half-tolerated consciousness
That plants its grammar in her yielding weather
But that unspeaking daughter, growing less
Familiar where we fell asleep together.

Wakeful moth-wings blunder near a chair,
Toss their light shell at the glass, and go
To inhabit the living starlight. Stranded hair
Stirs in the still linen. It is as though
The black breathing that billows her sleep, her name,
Drugged under judgment, waned and—bearing daggers
And balances—down the lampless darkness they came,
Moving like women: Justice, Truth, such figures.

Having remained inarticulate for most of my youth, I discovered more or less simultaneously the means of poetic expression and of honesty in love. For a time the two arts developed together so closely that only those poems succeeded which I wrote in the pursuit of love. Yet, while the matter of those poems was mine, much of their manner was drawn from other poets.

In "Another September," love achieved its object, the vein of love poems came to an end, and new themes began to be freed in a language which, I believe, shows traces of being my own.

Thomas Kinsella

Philip Levine

FOR FRAN

She packs the flower beds with leaves,
Rags, dampened papers, ties with twine
The lemon tree, but winter carves
Its features on the uprooted stem.

I see the true vein in her neck
And where the smaller ones have broken
Blueing the skin, and where the dark
Cold lines of weariness have eaten

Out through the winding of the bone.
On the hard ground where Adam strayed,
Where nothing but his wants remain,
What do we do to those we need,

To those whose need of us endures
Even the knowledge of what we are?
I turn to her whose future bears
The promise of the appalling air,

My living wife, Frances Levine,
Mother of Theodore, John, and Mark,
Out of whatever we have been
We will make something for the dark.

"For Fran" is my personal favorite among my poems because it says in an acceptable form what no man has a right to say to his wife. I married my wife for her beauty; not having any of my own, I was troubled and went in search of it. As in any improbable success story, things went badly at first, then worse, but ignorance and luck were finally rewarded.

I wanted to write a poem avowing my love for my wife, but I'm an essentially shy man, and beauty leaves me inarticulate. The years passed. I wrote poems about the torture of Algerians, about the history of the Jews, about the impoverished town we'd settled in, Fresno, California. Children came, handsome but unmanageable sons. The price they exacted was enormous, and my wife paid it. She paid it day by day, in her flesh and in her spirit.

For three months during the stifling summer of 1960 I worked without profit on a poem to my wife. One evening after the kids were in bed and the dishes were done and the thermometer still hung in the 100's I really looked at her. Like the Algerian Nationalist, like the homeless Jew, like the broiled cotton-picker of Fresno, she had become grist for the mill of my poetics.

A month later at the end of a decent day I had the courage to read her the completed poem. She wept with gratitude. She who never cried in pain wept real tears for these twenty inept lines that celebrate the curse of being a wife.

Philip Levine

Anne Sexton

SOME FOREIGN LETTERS

I knew you forever and you were always old,
soft white lady of my heart. Surely you would scold
me for sitting up late, reading your letters,
as if these foreign postmarks were meant for me.
You posted them first in London, wearing furs
and a new dress in the winter of eighteen-ninety.
I read how London is dull on Lord Mayor's Day,
where you guided past groups of robbers, the sad holes
of Whitechapel, clutching your pocketbook, on the way
to Jack the Ripper dissecting his famous bones.
This Wednesday in Berlin, you say, you will
go to a bazaar at Bismarck's house. And I
see you as a young girl in a good world still,
writing three generations before mine. I try
to reach into your page and breathe it back . . .
but life is a trick, life is a kitten in a sack.

This is the sack of time your death vacates.
How distant you are on your nickel-plated skates
in the skating park in Berlin, gliding past
me with your Count, while a military band
plays a Strauss waltz. I loved you last,
a pleated old lady with a crooked hand.
Once you read *Lohengrin* and every goose
hung high while you practiced castle life

in Hanover. Tonight your letters reduce
history to a guess. The Count had a wife.
You were the old maid aunt who lived with us.
Tonight I read how the winter howled around
the towers of Schloss Schwöbber, how the tedious
language grew ín your jaw, how you loved the sound
of the music of the rats tapping on the stone
floors. When you were mine you wore an earphone.

This is Wednesday, May 9th, near Lucerne,
Switzerland, sixty-nine years ago. I learn
your first climb up Mount San Salvatore;
this is the rocky path, the hole in your shoes,
the yankee girl, the iron interior
of her sweet body. You let the Count choose
your next climb. You went together, armed
with alpine stocks, with ham sandwiches
and *seltzer wasser*. You were not alarmed
by the thick woods of briars and bushes,
nor the rugged cliff, nor the first vertigo
up over Lake Lucerne. The Count sweated
with his coat off as you waded through top snow.
He held your hand and kissed you. You rattled
down on the train to catch a steamboat for home;
or other postmarks: Paris, Verona, Rome.

This is Italy. You learn its mother tongue.
I read how you walked on the Palatine among
the ruins of the palaces of the Caesars;
alone in the Roman autumn, alone since July.
When you were mine they wrapped you out of here
with your best hat over your face. I cried
because I was seventeen. I am older now.

I read how your student ticket admitted you
into the private chapel of the Vatican and how
you cheered with the others, as we used to do
on the Fourth of July. On Wednesday in November
you watched a balloon, painted like a silver ball,
float up over the Forum, up over the lost emperors,
to shiver its little modern cage in an occasional
breeze. You worked your New England conscience out
beside artisans, chestnut vendors and the devout.

Tonight I will learn to love you twice;
learn your first days, your mid-Victorian face.
Tonight I will speak up and interrupt
your letters, warning you that wars are coming,
that the Count will die, that you will accept
your America back to live like a prim thing
on the farm in Maine. I tell you, you will come
here, to the suburbs of Boston, to see the blue-nose
world go drunk each night, to see the handsome
children jitterbug, to feel your left ear close
one Friday at Symphony. And I tell you,
you will tip your boot feet out of that hall,
rocking from its sour sound, out onto
the crowded street, letting your spectacles fall
and your hair net tangle as you stop passers-by
to mumble your guilty love while your ears die.

My choice is mostly personal. My special loyalty to "Some Foreign Letters" stems from its dual outlook toward the past and the present. It combines them in much the same way that our lives do— closer to life than to art. It distills a time for me, a graceful innocent age that I loved but never knew. It is, for me, like a strange photograph that I come upon each time with a seizure of despair and astonishment.

"Some Foreign Letters" is a mixture of truth and lies. I don't feel like confessing which is which. When I wrote it I attempted to make all of it "true." It remains true *for me* to this day. But I will say that it was written to my great aunt who came to live with us when I was about nine and very lonely. She stayed with us until she had a nervous breakdown. This was triggered by her sudden deafness. I was seventeen at the time that she was taken away. She was, during the years she lived with us, my best friend, my teacher, my confidante and my comforter. I never thought of her as being young. She was an extension of myself and was my world. I hadn't considered that she might have had a world of her own once. Many years later, after her death, I found a bound volume of her letters from Europe. (My family were the type that bound letters in leather.) The letters are gay and intimate and tragic.

The final test of a poem often comes during a public reading. I have almost always read this poem during a "reading" and yet its impact upon me remains strong and utterly personal. I get caught up in it all over again. By the time I get to the last verse my voice begins to break and I, still the public poet, become the private poet who wrote the poem. Because "Some Foreign Letters" still puts a lump in my throat, I know that it is my unconscious favorite. I must always trust such a choice.

Anne Sexton

Thom Gunn

MY SAD CAPTAINS

One by one they appear in
the darkness: a few friends, and
a few with historical
names. How late they start to shine!
but before they fade they stand
perfectly embodied, all

the past lapping them like a
cloak of chaos. They were men
who, I thought, lived only to
renew the wasteful force they
spent with each hot convulsion.
They remind me, distant now.

True, they are not at rest yet,
but now that they are indeed
apart, winnowed from failures,
they withdraw to an orbit
and turn with disinterested
hard energy, like the stars.

One reason I like this poem is that I wrote it with such ease; it's one of the few I've ever finished in two or three days. The title, part of a line in *Antony and Cleopatra*, was once pointed out by a friend as an attractive title for a poem, and I kept it in mind, carrying it over from notebook to notebook for several years. I started writing the poem, finally, almost by chance, and once I had written the first line and a half, I knew exactly what I wanted it to be, in scope, in tone, in suggestiveness. With almost all my other poems I am aware of the missed chances, the space between the conception and its embodiment, but with this I am for once aware of them only as different names for the same thing.

Thom Gunn

John Hollander

ARISTOTLE TO PHYLLIS
For Rogers Albritton

(The fourteenth-century legend of Aristotle and the girl sometimes called Campaspe exemplified the frailty of pagan learning and the power of Amor. Represented in medieval sculpture by a beaming court-lady astride a solemn scholar, the story is later illustrated by a modish whore forcing a nasty old man to carry her piggyback in the work of Northern engravers like Urs Graf, Baldung Grien and Lucas Van Leyden around the turn of the sixteenth century. The speaker in this poem is a composite of the medieval cleric and the lascivious humanist of the later pictures. *Meden agan:* the famous "nothing in excess" of the Greeks.)

This chair I trusted, lass, and I looted the leaves
    Of my own sense and of clerks' learning, lessened
The distance towards the end of my allotted eyesight
    Over dull treatises on Reason and
Sensuality, learning very little about
    What can still happen on a summer morning.
Faint sea-breezes, when felt too far inland, sometimes
    Smack bone-deep, bruise marine depths, somersault
Into a flood of sick sea-longing. You walked past
    The window where my writing desk stands thick
And oaken, jammed against the mullioned lights, and where
    A pitch pine litters all my work with fragrance
Once too often. If all beauty is scale and order,
    Well then, the old man is unbeautiful
In outraging his age, that should be past all dancing,
    Playing all too well the infidel sage
Unwilling even to gamble on a Final Life

That is no sleep. And this being so, a simple
Country matter can be so urgent, and a piece
        Of tumble, bubbly breasts and trollopy
Lurch, can matter so much. So little can be said
        For you, except that you're alive. But such
A question, with the right wind freshening from the sea
        Blows back and forth across the mind: the bright
Emphatic mosses, furring the cracks along the garden
        Wall, trembling in the touch of breeze and blurring
The surface of the masonry, fill all the sight.
        But still, trained in restraint and reared in reason,
I sit at my desk, half in death, and staring down at
        A wide papyrus, silenced, blanched and deafened
To pleas for eloquence, its face pale with long darkness:
        Some other age must smash its last defense.
We're no historians; what's past has faded, died, and
        Lingers no more; and only its remains
Appear in patchworks of quotation, as in all
        The fussy, fretted centos that I have
Assembled from the poets. Even here (and you
        Must get the scribe who reads you this to show
Them all to you) the tessellated lines of one
        Whose greatest voyages involved the vessel
From which he dipped pale ink of an exotic nature
        Appear; but in my language all these sink
Into an earthier journey. A few swift rounds
        Under the evergreens outside; the fir
And box-hedge hiding us, clouds peering in the pool
        To view gardens reflected, and the yews
Along the wall waving green, encouraging brushes;
        Come, Phyllis, come; the miles I have been saving
Are for your travelling. Only in middle age
        Did *meden agan* amount to anything.

Come away! pass the mead again; and gathering
    Your thick skirts bellyward, lean back and lead
Me, simpering, outside into the garden. There
    As you throw up your leg to climb astride
My back, I'll dutifully munch the bit; then bottom
    To bottom, will the no-backed beast run, duly
Peripatetic at each mossy garden corner.
    Giddyap, good Doctor! If by chance the static
And pungent waters of the garden pool reveal
    Our natures to our eyes, it's all part of
The party, eh? Stammering, balanced, the master
    Of those who know, old staggerer, not bearing
A chubby giggling slut merely, but rather, like
    Some fabled, prudent beast that bears with it
Its water, nutriment or home, will carry then
    The bed he'll soon board. Underneath a tent
Of cherried branches ripening fast, I'll put you to
    The plow, and turn your furrows up, and Spring,
Spring will envelop all the air. From far across
    The wall a scent of distant pines will fall
Even as now it drops across my writing desk,
    Full of reports of distant life, and hopes
Regained, and projects floated on an unnavigable
    Future. And whether there will be a fated
Sea fight tomorrow, exploding, showering results
    On the ignoring water, or merely a plodding
And serious fool about to quarrel with a colleague
    Over what once I might have meant (devout
Enough, both of them, although never having learned
    The tongue I write in) cannot be told now.
But at the brink of the moment, mad, mad, for its coming,
    Our knowledge quickens, ripping at the garment
That cloaks the truth that will be. Let's get on with it,

The game in which the master turns the silly
Ass, straining for breath, arousing the outraged gales of
What should have been a season of calm weather.

"Aristotle to Phyllis" is a poem that I'm sure no one could really like as I do. It's too full of private jokes for myself alone, and even the meter and rhyme scheme were designed only to help me write the poem, not to work in any obvious way. The meter, by the way, is an adaptation in stressed scansion of the elegiac couplet in which the shorter second line rhymes with the middle of the first one (or rather, with its third accented syllable). The rhyme is buried, and acts solely as a constraint on my choice of words. The poem's atmosphere is Gothic Humanist, so to speak, and I doubt if very many people share my enthusiasm for it. The quote from Wordsworth in the last line and the bit about the sea-fight tomorrow were mostly for the benefit of a philosopher friend who had himself written on the subject of contrafactual conditionals in a controversy currently going among analytic philosophers. While the poem's subject is a general and public one (a spring-song), I was thinking throughout of Mallarmé's sonnet, "Brise Marine"; while I wanted to refer to it, I didn't want the allusions to interfere with the movement of the language of my own poem. So I buried them. The first line of my poem is a version of Mallarmé's first line: "Le chair est triste, hélas! et j'ai lu tous les livres." The sixth, seventh, ninth and tenth lines, as well as the title, of the French poem are all echoed, purely with respect to their sound, in my own poem at various points. Aristotle's advice to the girl to get help in reading his letter to her is well given. If the poem works, it works without the reader catching these allusions. I like this poem because it is self-indulgent.

John Holland

X. J. Kennedy

IN A PROMINENT BAR IN SECAUCUS ONE DAY

To the tune of "The Old Orange Flute"
or the tune of "Sweet Betsey from Pike"

In a prominent bar in Secaucus one day
Rose a lady in skunk with a topheavy sway,
Raised a knobby red finger—all turned from their beer—
While with eyes bright as snowcrust she sang high and clear:

"Now who of you'd think from an eyeload of me
That I once was a lady as proud as could be?
Oh I'd never sit down by a tumbledown drunk
If it wasn't, my dears, for the high cost of junk.

"All the gents used to swear that the white of my calf
Beat the down of the swan by a length and a half.
In the kerchief of linen I caught to my nose
Ah, there never fell snot, but a little gold rose.

"I had seven gold teeth and a toothpick of gold,
My Virginia cheroot was a leaf of it rolled
And I'd light it each time with a thousand in cash—
Why the bums used to fight if I flicked them an ash.

"Once the toast of the Biltmore, the belle of the Taft,
I would drink bottle beer at the Drake, never draft,
And dine at the Astor on Salisbury steak
With a clean tablecloth for each bite I did take.

"In a car like the Roxy I'd roll to the track,
A steel-guitar trio, a bar in the back,
And the wheels made no noise, they turned over so fast,
Still it took you ten minutes to see me go past.

"When the horses bowed down to me that I might choose,
I bet on them all, for I hated to lose.
Now I'm saddled each night for my butter and eggs
And the broken threads race down the backs of my legs.

"Let you hold in mind, girls, that your beauty must pass
Like a lovely white clover that rusts with its grass.
Keep your bottoms off barstools and marry you young
Or be left—an old barrel with many a bung.

"For when time takes you out for a spin in his car
You'll be hard-pressed to stop him from going too far
And be left by the roadside, for all your good deeds,
Two toadstools for tits and a face full of weeds."

All the house raised a cheer, but the man at the bar
Made a phonecall and up pulled a red patrol car
And she blew us a kiss as they copped her away
From that prominent bar in Secaucus, N. J.

Poems leave me grateful to them only if while in the making they are slow to let me in on their ultimate purposes. This one came on like that. It began without any planning on my part, as a few disconnected lines set down in notebooks over three or four years. By and by, as occasionally I reread these snippets (the phrase "tumble-down drunk," the images of the little gold rose and the cigar made of money), they started to cohere, until out stepped a fictive person who wanted to say them. She may have been prodded to step forth, I think, by my having read a ballade by John Heath-Stubbs, in which an old trull laments that "after death there's a judgment due." Anyway, whatever caused her to appear, she came as a surprise; and the piece gave me another surprise too when I showed it to Claire McAllister, who promptly decided it ought to be sung and pointed out its tune to me. Ever since then, I have been hoping to write more songs, fewer poems that are merely one-way conversations.

Perhaps this one seems close to me, too, because it is rooted in familiar country. At one time Secaucus was the spot in the New Jersey meadows where New York City's garbage used to be incinerated. Nowadays the air is sweeter there, but during the spring of 1951 when I was commuting to New York on the D. L. & W., every time the train started passing through Secaucus all the passengers, as if with a single will, would desperately slam the windows. I rather liked Secaucus for that. It was only there that any of us commuters ever sensed, for even that one moment, the slightest bit of mutual humanity.

X. J. Kennedy

Ted Hughes

PIBROCH

The sea cries with its meaningless voice,
Treating alike its dead and its living,
Probably bored with the appearance of heaven
After so many millions of nights without sleep,
Without purpose, without self-deception.

Stone likewise. Stone is imprisoned
Like nothing in the Universe.
Created for black sleep. Or growing
Conscious of the sun's red spot occasionally,
Then dreaming it is the foetus of God.

Over the stone rushes the wind,
Able to mingle with nothing,
Like the hearing of the blind stone itself.
Or turns, as if the stone's mind came feeling
A fantasy of directions.

Drinking the sea and eating the rock
A tree struggles to make leaves—
An old woman fallen from space
Unprepared for these conditions.
She hangs on, because her mind's gone completely.

Minute after minute, aeon after aeon,
Nothing lets up or develops.
And this is neither a bad variant nor a tryout.
This is where the staring angels go through.
This is where all the stars bow down.

Every poet has a few rooted intuitions, gifts of his nature, that are like the teeth with which he takes hold of the world. Most of his work is a mastication of his casual experience. But I choose this poem because it seems to be one of my teeth. A Pibroch is a piece of music for bagpipes, a series of variations "chiefly martial, but including dirges." No sound hits me so deeply as bagpipes. A familiar spirit is supposed to serve a family for generations, and I look on this poem as an heirloom.

Ted Hughes

Jay Macpherson

THE BEAUTY OF JOB'S DAUGHTERS

The old, the mad, the blind have fairest daughters.
Take Job: the beasts the accuser sends at evening
Shoulder his house and shake it; he's not there,
Attained in age to inwardness of daughters,
In all the land no women found so fair.

Angels and sons of God are nearest neighbours,
And even the accuser may repair
To walk with Job in pleasures of his daughters:
Wide shining rooms more warmly lit at evening,
Gardens beyond whose secrets scent the air.

Not wiles of men nor envy of the neighbours,
Riches of earth, nor what heaven holds more rare,
Can take from Job the beauty of his daughters,
The gardens in the rock, music at evening,
And cup so full that all who come must share.

Perhaps we passed them? it was late, or evening,
And surely those were desert stumps, not daughters,
In fact we doubt that they were ever there.
The old, the mad, the blind have fairest daughters.
In all the land no women found so fair.

This poem is valuable to me because it represents the apotheosis and monument of a personage called Jenny Lear, and says to the inquirer, usually me, that she is not dead but sleeping.

Jay Macpherson

Leonard Cohen

FOR ANNE

With Annie gone
Whose eyes to compare
With the morning sun?

Not that I did compare,
But I do compare
Now that she's gone.

I want to write and read poems filled with terror and music that change laws and lives. This isn't one of them. But it has stuck with me long enough, like a lucky stone, to suggest that it's true.

Leonard Cohen

Library of Congress Cataloguing in Publication Data

Poet's choice.
Reprint. Originally published: New York: Time Inc.,
c1962. (Time reading program special edition)
1. American poetry—20th century.   2. English poetry—20th century.
I. Engle, Paul, 1908-   .   II. Langland, Joseph.
III. Series: Time reading program special edition.
[PS614.P625 1982]   811'.5'08   82-663 AACR2
ISBN 0-8094-3714-7 (deluxe)
ISBN 0-8094-3715-5 (pbk.)